Voices of Romford

Voices of Romford

Patricia Pound

The History Press

Essex County Council Libraries

For B. An ideal husband

Frontispiece: A watercolour by well-known local artist David Millington of St Edward the Confessor Church in the Market Place, Romford, Essex. (© Millington)

First published 2008

The History Press Ltd
The Mill, Brimscombe Port
Stroud, Gloucestershire, GL5 2QG
www.thehistorypress.co.uk

British Library Cataloguing in Publication Data.
A catalogue record for this book is available from the British Library.

ISBN 978 0 7524 4758 2

Typesetting and origination by The History Press Ltd.
Printed in Great Britain

Contents

Acknowledgements

I would like to sincerely thank every one of the contributors to this collection of stories and memories of the past who willingly gave so generously of their time and also for the loan of their precious photographs. In the retelling and sharing of these memories they find an opportunity to present their story in order that others might know how the local population dealt with everyday events in and around the twentieth century. Some of the recollections are of happy highlights in their lives while others recall events and experiences which tested the spirit. These memories have remained imprinted on the mind of many individuals, never to be forgotten in their lifetime and here they share these experiences. In changing times, it is hoped that some of the community spirit and simple pleasures of the past may inspire a new generation to value this contribution from those who lived through these times and pass on their experiences for your consideration.

My special thanks must be expressed to David Clark in particular for invaluable introductions to many contributors, his own contributions and continual helpful advice. I also wish to recognize the usefulness of the *Romford Recorder* archive material available at the Central Library of Havering for research purposes.

Introduction

The county of Essex and the town of Romford in particular do not always enjoy a 'good press' but this book recalls the indomitable spirit of the people which still exists among the population today. An amalgamation of an established Essex rural stock combined with the cockney East Enders who spread out from London, then attracting a mobile society seeking work in the south-east of England and today accommodating a further mixture of migrants from many parts of the world. The twentieth century, in particular, was a time of immense change in society generally, new inventions and innovations bringing great changes to the lives of individuals; the progress made in all forms of transportation, from the bicycle to motor cars to aeroplanes through to a rocket on the moon. From the early days of photography to the digital age, and in communication from the telephone to satellite navigation, and from crystal set radio to television through to the wonders of cyberspace and computers.

The contributors to this book have experienced much of the history of these times; how the people of Romford celebrated the good times and survived the rest are recorded here. The willingness of the contributors to take part demonstrates that a spirit of goodwill still exists, with a combined pride and sense of place here in this famous market town. Others who have left the area were glad of the opportunity to record their affectionate memories of their former years spent in the town. This selection of stories from the past gives a snapshot of the everyday lives of the people who lived here in and around the twentieth century. This book, I trust, represents the voice of the people of Romford who lived and loved and shared and cared in this area through changing times, recorded here to entertain, educate and edify any former preconceived notions.

The comments on the highlights and low times in their lives are shared within the pages of this book giving a taste of how certain events would affect their lives. There are days of sadness and days of joy remembered here. It is a reflection of former times which have been documented in this way in order to preserve the memories for those who shared these decades and to give readers of the future an understanding of how people viewed these times. Since the year 2000, when we celebrated the new millennium, the people of Romford have witnessed another gigantic stride in the town's history. A continuing enormous redevelopment plan has been taking place providing a mix of office, retail, and residential housing (mostly one- and two-bedroom flats), changing the previously familiar face of Romford. This rebuilding even infiltrates into the old Romford Shopping Hall situated in the Market Place, undoubted long-term progress for the town but viewed with sadness by many former residents, as the Market Place now seems dwarfed by the high-rise buildings which surround it.

Stories involving the past, with reminiscences on the fond memories of their parents, childhood, schooldays, etc., are endowed with a special fondness and their own unique viewpoint. Personally, I found it enlightening and fascinating to hear these individual recollections relayed by those who experienced or heard them from a trusted source. The experience for me confirmed that the indomitable spirit of these people lives on, and a pride in the place they call home persists. Their memories seem to belong to a gentler time where days seemed longer, amusements less costly and life was lived at a more leisurely pace. There was an appreciation of the good things life offered, expectations were not so great and a belief in saving to afford was necessary in the days before the credit-card culture became the norm. Times change and a new generation carves another path into the future and once again newcomers to the area are bringing more and varied cultures to add to the local population.

It is hoped this book will bring back personal memories to those who were born and bred in Romford and have lived here throughout their lives, also to those who have travelled far and wide away from the town but still hold the place dear in their hearts. I trust newcomers will find it worthwhile and interesting to gain an understanding of the former life and times of this place and the people they are joining in the local population. It is hoped it will be constructive in providing information and knowledge of what it was to be a 'Romfordian' over the many decades and the loyalty this instilled in the local population.

One

School, Work and Play

The Factory School

My grandparents lived in Brentwood Road where they brought up a family of six children who all did well in their adult lives. My father was born just prior to 1900 and died in 1989. He had attended the Factory School and also the old Salisbury Road School. On leaving school his parents sent him to Parkinson's College in Balgores Lane. Education was high priority with my grandparents and evening classes and self-education was encouraged. I also attended Salisbury Road School in the 1930s. The headmaster at that time was Mr Hewlett who lived in a bungalow in Brentwood Road – he was a strict disciplinarian and never flinched in using the cane on unruly boys, me included! It is difficult to remember whether the introduction of milk was free or we paid a token price of a halfpenny for the dubious pleasure of sucking through ½pt full-cream milk. On a cold morning the memory of youngsters sucking and the bubbling noises as the last vestige of milk was drunk and the smell of it put me off milk for life. The playground was asphalt and any falls meant grazed knees or elbows and certainly no sympathy from parents. A dab of iodine brought forth more yells.

A Mr Buggs was one of my teachers and he took a bunch of us to the Natural History Museum in London. I carried the huge rucksack containing our lunches. One teacher delighted in humiliating me as I had a dyslexic approach to figure work – this was not sympathetically dealt with or recognised at the time. The class also used 'play money' during the lessons. It was just so much cardboard to me and my brain could not latch on to numbers. During holiday time my father, who was brilliant at figure work, used to set me addition and multiplication sums which had to be completed before his homecoming from the office. My so-called friends who wanted me to come out and play did not volunteer to help. My father used to set me other tasks such as weeding the paths during the school holidays. This introduction to gardening at such a young age must have had the right effect as gardening became one of my passionate pastimes. Back at Salisbury Road School again the caretaker was a lovely old boy, always in blue overalls and sported a great walrus moustache. He kept the boilers going and cleaned the lavatories which were pretty primitive but always smelled of carbolic. When I visit the school today, for example at voting time, the smell of the parquet floor brings back the memories. On leaving Salisbury Road School I went to Hylands School, a different and tough school where one learnt early on not to blub!

Chris Amis

A class of young children with their teachers at London Road School, 1947. (Lesley Godbold)

A group of young children at London Road School, 1950. (Lesley Godbold)

Coming to Romford

Dad came to Romford to work for the Ford Motor Co. He obtained work in the laboratories at Dagenham plant which became world famous for the Ford connections. The family roots had been in a Yorkshire village and this was a big move for the family. Coming to Romford from 'up north' in the early 1930s as a five year old, my handicap was that I spoke with a broad Yorkshire accent. The people 'down south' had difficulty understanding me. When I was sent to school at Crowlands Infants' School down the London Road, both children and teachers had trouble understanding me, for my accent was a curiosity you see. People did not move about the way they do today and had less knowledge of what was then thought of as 'foreign parts.' Having spent so long in Romford since that time there is no trace of my Yorkshire roots in my voice today. From that time I remember being able to play out in the street, as there was very little traffic about, mainly horse and cart deliveries. The milkman would serve milk from a milk churn and pour the required amount into your jug, using his special measures. The bread man also delivered to the door, either with a horse and cart or handcart. I had freedom when old enough to ride a bicycle to travel around the neighbouring countryside, for Romford was not built up as it is today. We had no television but listened to the radio or wireless set; my favourite programmes included the 'Ovaltinies Club.' I remember singing along to the Ovaltine song, which went something like this:

> We are the Ovaltinies, happy boys and girls,
> at work and play we all agree,
> no happier children can be seen
> because we all drink Ovaltine.
> We're happy boys and girls.

Judy Smith (*née*) Watters

Cabbage and Chalk Dust

The smell of cooking cabbage, of chalk dust and milk crates will always be with me, as will the images of children silhouetted against the distant sunlight in the cream and brown corridors of my Romford school. High drama was enacted in those classrooms and in those playgrounds. No one was indifferent, there were close friends and deadly enemies; the playground was a miniature world of rivalry and friendship, triumph and defeat. Mad, unthinking delight and abject misery. Shouts, shrieks, the scuffle of 'Blakies' boot studs on the asphalt, all brought to a precipitous halt at the blast of a whistle. For a long moment immobile, whistle poised as the teacher surveyed us. Then, at the second blast, a split second to conclude the interrupted conker or cigarette-card deal before the lines were formed and the ordered files moved purposefully towards the dreaded arithmetic or, joyous alternative on Friday afternoons, our teacher reading us another chapter of *Wind in the Willows* when our imaginations would wander drowsily from the dusty classroom to the languid reedy world of the river bank. On such afternoons, we almost resented the interruption of the hand bell which brought us back to reality, as the scuffling of feet and the banging of desk lids signified the end of yet another week and the prospect of the weekend to come.

Louis Roskell

Ignorance is Bliss

My fifth birthday was in July 1940. My brother, Bernard, came from school for his lunch and said that his headmistress, Miss Walker, had agreed that I could start school immediately. So without more ado, after lunch, I eagerly went back with him to Havering Road Primary School. No doting mother to accompany me, I was a big girl now. I can still remember sitting on the steps waiting for the bell to ring and the doors to open. However, it was not my first taste of school as I had been allowed to go with Bernard to a neighbour's house a couple of months before, when the neighbour, Mrs Frankham, held classes in her house because the school had closed due to the war. This did not last long and the children soon went back to school as normal.

As the war progressed, it was commonplace for us to see, as we walked to school along the Arterial Road, the British soldiers marching towards Gallows Corner. Or quite often it was the Americans in trucks. These were our favourites as they threw out handfuls of sweets, chewing gum and wrapped sugar lumps that we had never seen before. But whoever they were, we children would run alongside, waving and cheering and holding up our fingers in a 'V' for 'victory' sign. Except one day an elderly gentleman told me that I was holding my hand the wrong way round and it was not very nice. Oh well! Ignorance is bliss.

Hilda Bennett (*née*) Wilson

Scholarship Air Raid

In 1944 I sat the scholarship as it was called then, but later was known as the eleven-plus, and we all went to Dury Falls School in Hornchurch to sit the exam. The examination was held up for a time due to an 'air raid' and we all had to go into air-raid shelters in the playground. I do not recall being phased by this and we all took it in our stride – well, after all there was a war on! I passed the scholarship and went to Romford Intermediate School which a year later became known as Romford County Technical School. We had a massive playing field and the other feature I recall was that it was co-ed, meaning that there were girls in my class. This was a new experience and also a major distraction in class until the novelty wore off. I caught the No. 86a bus and travelled to Romford with some friends whom I had grown up with at junior school, two of whom I am still in touch with to this day – Paddy Brennan and Brian Hackshall. Paddy (now known as Pat) lives in Ireland and Brian in Wales. I am still the Essex boy I have always been. We used to walk together through the Market Place to our school and Wednesday was market day when the farmers brought lambs and pigs for trading. I used to hate hearing the pig squeals as they were branded, having their ears pierced and screaming so much I felt sure they were being killed. I continued at school until I was almost seventeen and was in the sixth form being prepared for matriculation. My aim was to do well as my father had arranged for me to be articled to a firm of accountants in London, so I needed matriculation as the School Certificate I had gained the previous year was not considered sufficient qualification. Unfortunately I failed one subject but did not want to stay on at school for another year to repeat the exam. My auntie kindly intervened and suggested I went into Westminster Bank as that was where uncle worked and if you liked figures that would be the right job. I was accepted after interview and started work on my seventeenth birthday. Banking served me well as a career but that is another story for another day.

John Saxton

Moss Lane Infants' School

In April 1943, just after my fifth birthday, Dad, a policeman, put me on the crossbar of his bicycle and we rode round the corner from Victoria Road into Albert Road then left into Moss Lane for my first day at school. That was the first of only two occasions on which I was ever taken to school in thirteen years. The second was when I was at the Romford County Technical School when I got a lift in a police car which happened to be going to Romford from Brentwood, where I then lived. Moss Lane Infants' School was presided over by the headmistress, a kindly old lady called Miss Howship. She must have been within a year or two of retirement because when my brother, John, arrived there three years later, she had been replaced by the stern Miss Sparkes. My first teacher was Miss Ferguson, who must have still been in her late teens because she still wore her Brentwood Ursuline High School blazer. There were pictures of birds around the classroom. I sat under the picture of the chaffinch. We were in awe of Miss Ferguson, because when she turned to the blackboard, she warned us that she had eyes at the back of her head. I tried many times to spot those all-seeing eyes hidden in her brown hair, but never did. We used slates to learn our alphabet, but Tommy Bennett used to amuse us by spitting on his and getting the deposit to draw patterns under the influence of gravity!

The four classrooms led off the main hall and the day started with assembly when we all marched into the hall, swinging our arms, to the strains of *Turkish Rondo* by Beethoven, played on the piano by Mrs Spencer. She was a tall lady with auburn hair and freckles who was always smiling. At the piano, she wore a navy-blue beret and raincoat, as first thing in the morning, the school was usually cold. Everybody liked her. I was never taught by her, but would gladly have swapped her for Miss Ferguson! There were metal lines screwed into the woodblock floor lengthways down the hall. We had to line our toes up against these while we recited the *Lord's Prayer* then sang a hymn, usually *All Things Bright and Beautiful* or *God is Love*. Lessons would be interspersed with games played either in the playground or in the hall. Favourites with the boys were *The Big Ship Sails Through the Alley, Alley Oo,* and *Tom Tiddler's Ground*. Favourites with

Class III at Mawney Road School, late 1920s. Second row, bottom right is Marjorie Thorogood. (Lesley Godbold)

the girls were *The Farmer's in his Den* and *Mary is A-weeping*. During the morning, we would be marched to the cloakroom where Mrs Gower, the milk-and-dinner lady, would dole out the regulation ⅓pt milk. At the end of the day, Miss Ferguson would order, 'Stand. Lines', and we would sing *Now the Day is Over*. Then, the longed-for hour of quarter-to-four, when we would stream out into Moss Lane and get clear of the school before the 'big kids' came out of the adjoining junior school in Albert Road at four o'clock.

David Clark

Destination Romford

When my father came back from the war he was posted to London with the Transport Police, so we moved from our village in Norfolk to Romford. Eight years old at the time I attended Mawney Road School. The first few weeks there were to say the least quite a challenge. Things

Romford County Technical School, 1950s, with Hilda Wilson second row, centre. (Hilda Bennett)

were a bit difficult for a village 'country boy' arriving from Norfolk with a pronounced accent. At first the other children found it very amusing to laugh at my accent and claimed they often could not understand what I was saying, however, thankfully this did not last long and I was soon accepted. At eleven, after the scholarship tests, I transferred to Pettits Lane School, where I remember having the 'cane' whacked across my hand a few times. This was a very normal event in those days and does not indicate that I was especially badly behaved. Until you had the cane at school you were not considered 'one of the boys.' Looking back on those days I have to admit that I enjoyed a very happy and carefree childhood in Romford.

Ron Fuller

Moving On

Aged eleven, I left Havering Road Junior School and went up to Pettits Lane Senior School. Aged thirteen, I entered what was called the late-developers' exam. This I passed and went on to the Romford Country Technical School or the Intermediate School, as it was sometimes called, to finish my education. This included shorthand and typing lessons and for this we had to walk down Marshall's Drive to Marshall's Hall, which had recently been acquired by the school. We felt very important as we sat in these grand rooms with their lofty ceilings, so different from normal school, which was ruled by the headmaster, Mr Church. I was always one for doing acrobats and one day Mr Church caught my friend and I doing handstands up the wall in the playground, which he said was very unladylike. Our punishment was to stand at the top of the stairs outside his office, one in each corner every lunchtime break. It did not take us long to take a ball with us to while away the time playing 'catch.'

Hilda Bennett (*née*) Wilson

Albert Road Primary

Albert Road Primary School was presided over by the fearsome headmaster, Mr Cocker. He spent most of his time upstairs in his study. We always saw him on Friday mornings before school when he conducted his weekly canings. He did this in the playground in the summer and in the hall in the winter. His victims were invariably boys from the Cottage Homes at Hornchurch. Not that they were any worse than us. They just had no parents to take their part. We were lined up in silence in the playground or the hall and we could hear Mr Cocker coming down the uncarpeted wooden stairs from his study. He would slap his cane against his thigh and shout, 'Haddap' (Heads Up!) when he came into view. Then the unfortunate boys, usually Peter Bangs and George Ashton, would be called out and given a thrashing on their backs, legs or bottoms. Once Peter made a run for it, but he was given a pasting, once Mr Cocker cornered him. The Cottage Homes' boys were delivered every morning in a green single-decker bus. Before the war they were accompanied by a man in a uniform looking like Mr Bumble, the beadle in *Oliver Twist*. There were also girls from the Scattered Homes orphanage in Carlisle Road.

In 1945, the school had six classes: Class 6 was a remove for slow learners and presided over by Miss Nash. She was a smart lady in her fifties who brooked no nonsense. She always wore her black hair in a chignon. Class 5's teacher was Miss John, one of the many Welsh teachers who moved to England at that time. She was short and dark, quietly spoken and a very good teacher. Class 4 was another remove for older, slow learners. Some children spent the whole of

David Clark, pupil at Albert Road School, 1940s. (David Clark)

their four years in junior school in the two remove classes. Miss Taylor was in charge. She was a slight, old-fashioned, maiden lady, who fascinatingly had the top of one of her index fingers missing. She ran the school choir and took us to St Edward's Church in Romford Market Place for the school's carol service at Christmas and to the school's choirs' competition held at Pettits Lane Secondary School in the spring term. Both events were presided over by Dr Swinburne who now has a hall named after him at Colchester Institute. Miss Taylor left for Australia while I was at Albert Road and was replaced by Mr Phillips, another Welshman.

Mrs Baker looked after Class 3. She was another good teacher who had a son at Brentwood School, who sometimes came in to help his mother in class. We all used to look forward to the stories she read just before home time. Class 2 was where we really started to work in preparation for the eleven-plus. Some of us were fast forwarded from Class 2 to Class 1 so that we could spend four or five terms in the top class before taking the all-important exam. Mr Huntley was in charge of Class 2. He was ex-RAF and had spent the war in Malta. He made a speciality of geography and had been to a number of places we learned about and made us want to go there one day. He bought one of the first ballpoint pens, a Biro. We all went up to his desk one day and ceremoniously signed our names with it. I found that it slipped all over the place and produced 'stripy' writing. Mr Huntley was Welsh and came from Mountain Ash. Eventually, he took over Class 1 and then became headmaster when Mr Cocker retired.

Class 1, the eleven-plus hothouse, was the domain of the unforgettable Mr Baines. In 1949, when he got me together with several others, through the exam, Mr Baines was one year

Prefects and teachers at Romford County Technical School, 1956. Front row, left to right: Sandra Weevers (deputy head girl), Coryn Bird (head girl), Mr H.V. Church (headmaster), Miss A. Skipsey, (senior mistress), Eleanor Lanning. Middle row: -? -, -? -, -? -, Sheila Brown, Sheila Rolfe, Blanch Gover, -? -, -? -, Back row: -? -, Glennis Owens, Margaret Millar, -? -. (Glennis Keeley)

away from retirement. He had taught some of the parents of his class of 1949. You worked hard and inattention was rewarded with a smart crack of his short cane across your shoulders. No surprise then when we chanted on leaving school on the last day of term, 'Mr Baines ain't got no brains, but he's got a lot of canes!' He was a martyr to colds and in winter he usually had a dewdrop on the end of his nose. All the class waited for it to drop off! Nevertheless, he made every subject interesting and we all grudgingly admired him. He was assisted by the auburn-haired Mr Smedmore, who was, again, ex-RAF aircrew, and would pepper his lectures with 'wizard show!' or 'you're off the beam!' In all, Albert Road Primary was a very good school for the brighter pupils. Every year, a dozen or so of the class of 1949, all now seventy or near, hold a reunion to celebrate those happy, far-off years.

David Clark

Cricket Teas and Catering

I did not pass the eleven-plus although I felt I was quite bright, but practical rather than academic. However they accepted me at the Romford County Technical School after an interview. After an initial period of being a problem with high spirits and insubordination, I settled down to maths, geography, cookery and dressmaking lessons. My excess energy was directed towards helping with the cricket teas and catering for the drama evenings and sports

Prefects and masters at Romford County Technical School, 1956. Front row, left to right: Johnny Butterworth (deputy head boy), David Clark (head boy), Mr H.V. Church (headmaster), Mr Sinclair (senior master), John Head. Middle row: Barry Cappi (who became captain of Romford Football Team, when they were in the fourth division in the 1960s), Jackaman, -? -, -? -, -? -, -? -, Gower, -? -. Back row: ? Wright, Dave Wilkinson, Ray Ilott, Les Cameron. (David Clark)

days. That kept me out of mischief most weekends and some evenings. I did not know what I wanted to do, so I was allowed to try technical drawing – not careful enough; then shorthand and typing – alright, but not my life; economics – interesting but not exciting; teaching – no; probation officer – no, needed a degree. Eventually I became a nursing sister and midwife, a worthwhile choice of career. What chances I had and what effort the staff at the school put in to find me a place in life! Looking back I value the school and the teachers for giving me chances and responsibilities and was proud to be made head girl, which raised my self-esteem. They also gave me the opportunity to join a couple of lovely trips to Austria, Germany and Switzerland, climbing and walking in the mountains. I still struggle with languages, including English! But I would like to take this opportunity to say a big thank you, to the former Romford County Technical School, which played such an important part in my life.

Coryn Hart (*née*) Bird
Head Girl, Romford County Technical School 1956/57

End of an Era

You could never miss the Romford County Technical School in Romford Market Place at 4.15 p.m. on a weekday. The Market Place was awash with boys and girls all wearing their red caps and hats. No wonder we were known locally as the 'red-hat' school. The school started off in the 1920s as the Romford Intermediate School in Mawney Road and the first headmaster was Mr Maskelyne. The idea was that children who passed the eleven-plus should have the opportunity to be educated to prepare them for careers in industry and commerce, rather than other professions, which had traditionally placed emphasis on the classics. In the 1930s the school moved to new premises in Havering Drive, under the headship of Mr H.V. Church, BA, and like other such schools all over the country, it became a technical school. For the first three years, pupils studied traditional subjects, then they must decide which 'side' we would be on for the rest of our school career – technical or commercial and in that year we were able to sample every course on offer during that last term. In the 1950s the technical side offered engineering drawing, metalwork, applied maths, physics and chemistry and later design and technology. The commercial side offered bookkeeping, shorthand, typing and biology. Both sides carried on with English, French, geography, art and other core subjects. We were told that if you 'put your back into it' you could achieve any goal. The technical side produced students who became engineers in industrial concerns such as Ford Motor Co. and the then thriving aircraft industry; others pursued technical careers in the Royal Air Force, the Royal Navy and the Merchant Navy. Many who went on to university entered Oxford and Cambridge. The school also produced doctors who were coached in Latin and chemistry by dedicated teachers in their spare time. My contemporaries between 1949 and 1956 who left school and made good included the art director of Penguin Books who converted the covers from orange-white, orange-green, white-green to the illustrated covers used today. He then became an illustrator for the Beatles and numerous children's books. Another became the financial director of Ford of Europe.

Not only was the teaching good, we were taught what to expect on leaving school because most of the technical and commercial staff had been recruited from industry and commerce. Our engineering-drawing master was a naval architect and our applied maths and metalwork master was a ballistics specialist. We were also taught the best way to approach business negotiations with people from the eastern hemisphere and how to hold a conversation during an unexpected encounter with royalty. Both of these skills I had to recall and use in later life.

Although I was on the technical side and subsequently followed a career in radar and computer engineering, I took A-level French. I was allocated a place at the Paris Easter School at the Lycee Condorcet in Paris and for two weeks I stayed with a French family who spoke no English and with whom I am still in contact, fifty-two years later! I still use French as chairman of the committee which deals with Billericay's twin town of Chauvigny.

The school's only concession to Latin was its motto, *Esse Quam Videri* – 'To be and not to seem', or as we were told, forget appearances and be yourself. This has stayed with me throughout life, as I am sure it has for many an ex-red hat. When the school finally closed in the 1990s and the land was sold off for a housing estate, 800 former pupils gathered for a final get together to pay tribute to a school and its staff, past and present, who, for over sixty years, had taught us in such a dedicated way and prepared us so well for life.

David Clark

Head Boy, Romford County Technical School 1955/56

Romford County High

When I passed the thirteen-plus examination and was to go to Romford County High it was a very exciting time. I can remember going with my mother to a tailor's shop in Victoria

Jean Williams cycles to Romford County High School, 1950s. (Jean Pound)

On stage at Romford County High School, March 1953. Left to right: Sheila Weevers, Patricia Cook, Susan Bartholomew, Elizabeth Kemp. (Jean Pound)

Road, Romford, to be measured for my school uniform for the start of term. This proved to be the beginning of a great opportunity as far as my education was concerned, and the valued friendships formed there have in some cases proved to be of lifelong duration. There were many happy years spent pedalling on my bicycle to and fro from school wearing my green uniform and memories of the school buildings abound. I enjoyed my schooldays and my favourite subjects were art and biology, although I hated hockey and somehow often managed to tidy the games shed instead. I enjoyed taking part in many of the various productions as a backstage worker, not for me the 'treading of the boards!' We staged *Hiawatha*, *She Stoops to Conquer* and many more. I was very definitely backstage busily involved in painting scenery and costume sewing, all helpful to the final production. I remember too the Christmas concerts and the sixth-form socials when the Royal Liberty boys were invited to join us, the staff standing sentinel around the hall! There were various special outings too and I remember visits to Horham Hall, Audley End and Canterbury together with theatre visits and I especially remember going to the Old Vic to see *Romeo and Juliet* with the beautiful young Claire Bloom playing Juliet. Another and most special outing was to the Festival of Britain in 1951 which was the famous and not to be missed exhibition, constructed on the south bank of the river, the Royal Festival Hall the only reminder remaining today. All happy memories of my time spent at Romford County High School. The school formed the foundation of a later career in education as a teacher and headmistress in the county of Essex prior to my retirement.

Jean Pound (*née*) Williams

An Important Interview

A successful examination result earlier in the year led to an interview at Romford County High School to confirm a place, in that impressive building set in leafy grounds, the Grammar School. As a sixth former led the way along impressive corridors, I glanced through an open door to the magnificent hall with gleaming parquet floor. All was quiet except for the clicking of chalk on the blackboards and teachers' measured tones in the classrooms as we passed. My heart missed a beat as I approached the sole chair facing the selection board, five elegant ladies and one clergyman all watching me intently. The questions now answered had been delivered with kindness and so my nervousness gradually subsided. At last, the black-robed headmistress thanked me and gave me leave to go. With relief I headed for the door when the floor came up and hit me in the face. Covered in confusion I apologised, my inquisitors showing genuine concern and then they smiled broadly as I left the room. Whether they sympathised and awarded my place as compensation I shall never know. I was almost bursting with pride when the letter came inviting me to attend the following term. My mother went to work to buy the uniform and I had my aunt's hand-me-down wool coat, dyed bottle green instead of the regulation gabardine raincoat. I carried my books in my leather music case until the funds ran to a satchel that Christmas. To this day, I am still very proud to have shared a little of the world of Romford County High School guided by the elegant and wise Miss Chappel and her admirable staff who gently moulded us into young ladies. Now fifty-eight years on, I still treasure my memorabilia of my school days and the memories of my teachers. Miss Eleanor Parker, head of French studies, so gentle and kind, although at a prize giving she confessed her surprise that I had squeezed a pass mark in my French 'O' level! Formidable Dr Hall, an awesome figure striding the corridors with black-silk gown billowing about her, realising I was a hopeless cause at logarithms, relegated me to the arithmetic class. Miss Gurr, enthralled

Edna Stickland and Jean Williams at the Festival of Britain, 1951. (Jean Pound)

Romford County High School for Girls with two pupils in the foreground, 1950s. (Jean Pound)

with her stories of all the world faiths in her religious-instruction class. Miss Stewart coaxed some creativity out of me in her English class. I am thankful for introduction to the world of Shakespeare, Dickens and Wordsworth and many more. Miss Pegrum presided over the science laboratory, Bunsen burners, pipettes and retorts. While Miss Laurenson taught the practical science of needlework and inevitably the art of patience when it took a whole term to complete one item. Beautiful Miss Miller instructed us in physical education, Miss Alderton's domestic-science room was a haven, smelling of the cakes and biscuits baked there. Miss Smith was undoubtedly my favourite – in her art studio we learnt to draw and reproduce accurately what we saw. This is a skill that has remained with me all my life. The school motto 'Gladly Lerne and Gladly Teche' was revived when I entered into teacher-training college many years later and taught at junior school for a few years. However, my special pal at school, Jean Williams, and my cousin, Doreen Stickland, both went on to successful teaching careers, becoming head teachers in their respective schools. I am very proud of them. I have no doubt that school days are the happiest days of our lives. Mine were those spent at the Romford County High School.

Edna Stock (née) Stickland

Our Playtime

My mother was widowed not long after the First World War and, for my siblings and I, life was going to be restricted in many ways. However we were a close and happy family and we children went to school locally and enjoyed our outdoor playtime as we grew up. For skipping you only needed a suitable length of rope, even an old washing line would do. Marbles and five stones also provided cheap amusement. A whip and a spinning top was another favourite. Hoops too, although if I remember rightly our 'hoop' was an old bike wheel. The boys concocted their designer 'trollies' made of any bits and pieces they could find. Orange boxes were greatly prized and used in many ways, including the manufacturing of household furniture in the form of storage cupboards etc., these were often obtained from the Market Place. Most of all, for the things we did not have we became inventive and our imaginations served us well in all our games and undertakings

We children all left school at fourteen to find work and offered to help with money for the family purse; we were a very close-knit family and helped each other. My own employment embraced some familiar factory names at the time: Lacrinoid, where I made buckles and belts, Plessey and the Roneo Works. A great deal has changed over the years and I am sorry to say in my opinion not always for the better. I know older people are accused of seeing the past through rose-coloured spectacles but the times, hard as they sometimes were, were 'the good old days' when families and neighbours worked together.

Ellen Whitehead (née) Shelley

Saturday Morning Pictures

There were three cinemas with a Saturday Morning Pictures Club: the Havana Odeon, the Gaumont Plaza and the ABC Ritz. I was a member of the Havana Odeon Club and my membership number was 0004. The manager's children were 0001 and 0002 and my sister was 0003. It appears the police station was canvassed for members first and our Dad was a policeman there. We paid 9d for a seat in the circle and the stalls were 6d. We queued up on the north wall of the cinema opposite some open ground behind the Como Ice-Cream Parlour. Once in, we were kept in order by the maroon-uniformed commissionaires and usherettes. One of the commissionaires sported Boer War medals on his chest, the same as my great uncle Harry.

The programme was always the same. Before the first film we bellowed our heads off with community singing, usually the old music hall favourites like *A Bicycle Made for Two* and *My Old Man Says Follow the Van*. The last one was Tommy Handley leading the Odeon song, *We come Along on Saturday Morning* with a white ball bouncing along the top of the words. The first film was a cartoon, usually Donald Duck losing his temper, then a fifteen-minute interest film. This could range from something like *How Rose Hip Syrup is Made* to Benjamin Britten's excellent *Young Person's Guide to the Orchestra*. Then an instalment of a serial and these were usually ancient, grainy, cowboy serials like *Riders of Death Valley*, or *Menace of the Deep* where giant octopi, sharks and other sundry scaly horrors threatened our underwater hero. Then, the main film – half of them were westerns featuring old favourites like Roy Rogers, Bill Boyd, Tex Ritter, Gene Autry, Johnny Mack Brown and Renfrew of the Royal Mounted Police. Their main failing for we boys was that, whenever they met a girl they would burst into song and hold up the action! Westerns always ended in a chase with heroes in white hats on white horses, going hell for leather after baddies in black hats on black horses, around Monument Valley.

At noon we poured out into South Street and made a beeline for Como's Ice-Cream Parlour. Cornets were 3d and wafers were 4d. I remember a bewildered old lady caught in the yelling maelstrom of children released from the Havana saying to her companion: 'It must be a Sunday-school treat.' Sunday school it wasn't, but treat it certainly was!

David Clark

Hilda Wilson skipping in the street with friends in Essex Road, 1950s. (Hilda Bennett)

Street Games

Unlike today, there was not much traffic about when I was a child – consequently it was not dangerous to play in the street. We had a field right opposite our house in Essex Road, where we played rounders, football, cricket and other ball games. There was also the opportunity to climb trees and to indulge in showing off our skills doing acrobats. I loved acrobats and displayed my skill at somersaults with cartwheels, back-bends the crab, leapfrog and performing 'aeroplanes,' where I would swing the smaller children round and round holding them by one arm and one leg. Nobody came out to tell us it was dangerous, we just knew what we were doing and nobody got hurt. We used the street for such games as 'tin-can Tommy' when we put a can in the centre of the road with crossed sticks on top. With a team on each side of the road the art was to knock the sticks off the can with a ball and then run, whereby the other team had to catch you. If we wanted to play 'house' there were always things around from bombed-out premises that we could use, such as pots and pans and bits of corrugated iron for walls. Skipping was also a good pastime with either two turning the rope for one in the middle or solo to see how many 'bumps' you could do. My house had an alleyway at the side and therefore the side of the house was ideal for playing 'two-balls'. We had lots of songs that we sang as we juggled the balls against the wall. I can remember *'One, Two, Three Alairy, Four, Five, Six Alairy,'* but please do not ask me the meaning of 'alairy' for I have no idea! When I was a bit older, maybe twelve or thirteen years old, my friends and I showed off our expertise at ballroom dancing in the centre of the road. This we had learned from older brothers and sisters and we would dance round and round and spin and twirl, singing our hearts out. This was all such innocent fun but so enjoyable, and I sometimes feel so sorry for the children of today with all the restrictions imposed upon them.

Hilda Bennett (née) Wilson

Happy Days

After the Second World War ended, my parents, Daisy and Bert Huggett, were thrilled when they were offered rehousing on the newly constructed estate at Harold Hill and I remember happy days for the family when we lived there. My Dad loved his garden and I remember him working there for hours it seems on his neat and scented flowerbeds, which seemed to me to be almost constantly in bloom. My brother Alex and I were allowed to play street games with friends and we were quite safe then for few families owned cars and the streets were fairly free of traffic. Alex and I went to Quarles School and I remember many outings and family treats during the school holidays; we especially liked to take a trip to Bedfords Park and visit the deer herd there in their enclosure. Open countryside was near at hand for visits to Havering-atte-Bower village, or out to Abridge and Theydon Bois and beyond to Epping Forest, and these places still offer attractive and popular sites to visit even today. Eventually my parents moved to Gidea Park and my husband and I to Brentwood but I remember with great affection the years of my growing up in and around Romford.

Ellen Preston (née) Huggett

Ellen Hugget and brother Alex in their front garden at Harold Hill. Note not a car in sight in the roadway. (Ellen Preston)

The deer herd at Bedfords Park – Ellen and brother Alex from Harold Hill were regular visitors. (Ellen Preston)

I Started Crying

I was born in 1938 and during the war we lived in Squirrel's Heath Lane, about a half mile from my school in Ardleigh Green. My brother, who is three years older than me, and I were evacuated to Wales for about six months, but were brought home before the following episode at school. I think the date of the V2 rocket as I have been told was around 25 or 26 January 1945. We had just finished registration in the classroom and were settling down to the first lesson when there was a sudden huge explosion. I can remember the windows being blown in and the ceiling coming down in a cloud of plaster dust. The teacher told us to get down under the desks where we crouched until told to get up again. We were formed up into lines and marched into the air-raid shelters standing in the playground. I started crying at this stage as I thought my mother had been killed! When we were later sent home and I walked towards my house to my dismay, some of the houses had their windows blown out by the blast but I could see my mother standing at the gate looking anxiously towards the school, so imagine my relief as I hurried home to her. Other wartime memories are of my brother and I looking for shrapnel on our way to school. At night, when the air-raid siren sounded I remember getting into the Morrison shelter, which we used as a dining table. My father would put on a steel helmet and sit at the table 'doing his books' for the shop whilst we all crouched inside.

Anthony Keeley

The Freeze of 1947

The winter of 1946–1947 was a grim time for Romford and indeed the whole country, but for we children, it was a time of pure bliss. There was thick snow which settled and never seemed to melt into slush, which meant that we could build snowmen in the garden and have friendly snowball fights with our friends. Mind you, we had to keep out of the way of rival gangs as we discovered to our cost that they put stones in their missiles. We learned to do the same when necessary and soon they became wary of us.

Sometimes our schools were closed when the central-heating pipes burst and this only added to our leisure time. The lake in Raphael Park froze over and hundreds of people would gather there in the evening to slide and skate. We made long slides near to the bank, but an area over towards the gardens in Lake Rise was roped off for the serious skaters. My brother and I went there on his sixth birthday, 25 February 1947, and we were fascinated to see people skating with real skates and not colliding with each other. We had seen Sonja Henie doing it at the cinema, but this was the real thing!

David Clark

The Havana Club

During the Second World War it was arranged that the local cinemas would open their doors on a Saturday morning for the children to see their very own films. So for 6d we all trooped in to see, firstly, the bouncing ball along the words as we all sang *Is everybody happy, YES*, then a cartoon would follow with the screams of delight at the antics of Mickey Mouse & Co., always a favourite, followed by the magic of a film about the famous dog Lassie or Roy Rogers with his horse Trigger or some other film suitable for children. But of course, the show always ended

Late 1940s and the gang's all here! The neighbourhood children would gather outdoors together for all kinds of games and adventures. (Derek 'Del' Osborne)

with an episode of a serial with a 'hold your breath' thrilling cliffhanger to make sure you came back next week. Before we went home we would visit Romford Market, with its colourful stalls and stallholders, shouting to sell their wares, made more exciting of course if we had a penny or tuppence to spend. Usually this was our bus fare home, but we did not mind the walking!

Hilda Bennett (*née*) Wilson

Beyond Romford

Weekends were a time of adventure and exploration with the advent of the bicycle, which Dad bought for me from Harry's bicycle shop at the top of the Market Place opposite the Laurie Cinema. With the aid of my *Geographia Cyclist Map*, my world began to extend beyond Bedfords Park and Havering village. One hot summer day George Wilson, Dickie Weaver and I actually reached distant Dunmow and how foreign it seemed to us. There was a railway station with a goods yard and a 'flitch' bacon factory, although we were not sure about 'flitches.' There was also a pub called the Kicking Dickie. Yes, we mused, there was civilisation beyond Ongar and it was a long way home to tea. For although Essex was close to London on its south-eastern corner it was also rural and remote: The Rodings, the Bumpsteads, Arkesden, Finchingfield and Thaxted were a world away from the factories and grime of the metropolitan area. Essex had long, hot, straight country lanes with ripening wheat, humming telephone wires and warm

Tizer to drink from funny-shaped bottles. Essex was wide summer skies with the occasional thunderstorm to contrast iron-dark cloud against white weatherboard and thatch.

Louis Roskell

Train Spotting

Train spotting was one of the passions of our boyhood. It seems incredible now that so much pleasure could be had just noting down the numbers and names of locomotives that passed. But it was not just that: it was the exhilarating noise and smell of smoke and steam, which has now all but passed into history. Everyone had his favourite spot and mine was the footbridge, which links Victoria Road with Junction Road. From the footbridge, you could look right down the funnels of passing trains and the smoke and steam would envelope you. Later, probably because annoyed mums were fed up with their little boys coming home grimy and smelling of smoke, barriers were put on the sides of the bridge so that you could not even see the trains. There were four main railway lines and a branch line on the south side – this was the London Midland Scottish line which linked Romford with Emerson Park. This branch line had one train, which shuttled backwards and forwards between the two stations. The train had three, red third-class carriages and was pulled or pushed by a venerable old Victorian locomotive known locally as 'Puffing Billy.' This engine was a 0-4-0 and had an enormously tall funnel and a dome behind it almost as tall. We lived by the railway line and on foggy mornings would hear the detonators warning Puffing Billy that he was approaching Romford Station. Of the four main lines, the two outer ones carried local traffic from Liverpool Street to Shenfield. We had seen all the local ones many a time and collecting their numbers became even more boring when the line was electrified in the late 1940s and the trains appeared just to be carriages only! The two tracks in the middle were the ones we really kept our eyes on for they carried the express trains to Ipswich and beyond. The engines that pulled these trains were known to us as 'Sandies' – the tracks had long troughs of water between the rails so that the locomotives could take on water without stopping. Some of the 'Sandies' were 'Namers' and this meant that there was a plate on each side of the engine with perhaps the name of a famous person or a regiment. At one stage, there were American lease-lend locomotives to be seen, but they did not impress; black and covered with pipes, valves, air horns, huge lamps and cowcatchers, not at all like our beautiful streamlined British ones. When no trains were passing, there was plenty of mischief we could get up to! The boldest among us would hop over the railings and put a penny or a halfpenny on Puffing Billy's nearest rail while another put his ear to the rail to listen for an approaching train. It was quite a trophy – a halfpenny that had been flattened to the size of a penny by Puffing Billy! Another trick, which only one boy to my knowledge dared to do, was to lay between the track and let puffing Billy pass over him! The rest of us were content just to take train numbers.

David Clark

Peter Pan's Playground

In the 1950s I attended school at St Mary's Convent School in Western Road, Romford, and often my mother and stepfather used to collect me from school and we would drive down the A127 – Arterial Road to Southend-on-Sea. What a treat! We always arrived in time to spend

Pauline Baker at Westcliff-on-Sea, photographed with live monkey, 1950s. (Pauline Hollingsworth)

awhile at Peter Pan's Playground before it closed. I used to love the 'House That Jack Built' and enjoyed all the amusement offered at this favourite venue for children. Afterwards we would go to a small tearoom, and I think it was called the Copper Kettle, to enjoy a cream tea. This was a regular, weekly trip on sunny summer afternoons and I looked forward to these visits with great anticipation. Southend was a destination considered by everyone around as 'the seaside' – a place for enjoyment of every kind, from the Kursaal to the amusement arcades along the front, to train rides out to the end of the pier, that famous longest pier in the world! But for me at that time, Peter Pan's Playground was paradise.

Pauline Hollingsworth (*née*) Baker

Games we Played

In the area around Albert Road and Victoria Road there was not a lot of space for playing games. Albert Road Junior School had no playing field so we had no opportunity to be taught football or cricket. The only places we could go to were the Roneo Sports Ground at the end of Park Lane or Hylands Park. There, we would kick a tennis ball around using piles of coats as a goal. It was not so much Association Football we played, more an extended version of street warfare, as we practiced the art of 'hocking' – disabling your opponent by kicking his ankles. It has not escaped my notice that, sixty years later, 'hocking' is now not unknown in the Premier Division. I eventually acquired a proper football, which gave me high status in the street hierarchy. I also had a couple of cricket bats and a set of stumps, which the family used to play with on the beach in summer holidays and we boys used these in Hylands Park. We had our own rules, one of which I remember was that you could avoid being run out if you yelled, 'save time', before you got back to the crease. We did play a version of cricket at Albert Road School which used stumps chalked on the wall. One boy called Sidney Needs was very good at it and once he was in nobody could get him out.

It was no wonder that when I got to the Romford County Technical School I was ignorant of the rules of either football or cricket and consigned to cross-country and swimming for the duration. Somehow it was expected that little boys magically acquire that knowledge at birth.

Our really favourite games we played in the playground at Albert Road. Which elderly pensioner has never played 'Hi Jimmy Nacker?' Two teams mostly of six – one were horses and the other were riders – and one boy acted for both teams and he was the post. The post was usually someone who was not allowed or unable to play rough games, a way of keeping less-fortunate mates involved. With his back to wall the post waited as the first horse put his head between the post's legs. Each of the horses put his head between the legs of the horse in front forming a line. Each rider then took a running jump and vaulted on the horses' backs. When all the riders were on the horses they then had to do their best to make the horses collapse, the horses trying to buck the riders off their backs while the riders chanted 'Hi Jimmy Nacker One, Two, Three', three times. If the horses collapsed the riders had won and the cry went up, 'weak horses.' The horses won if any part of the rider touched the ground.

Real fights occurred spontaneously in the playground, usually before school in the mornings and afternoons when no teachers were supervising us. Two boys would square up to each other and the cry, 'fight! fight!' began; everyone then gathered round cheering them on. However there were strict rules and everyone obeyed, no hitting below the belt, no kicking and no challenge to any who wore spectacles. Any of these offences would nickname you 'kick donkey' throughout your time at Albert Road Primary. I remember a fight where one of the boys was so busy punching away at his opponent he did not notice his short trousers had fallen down! The fights would be stopped by a member of staff, alerted by the commotion in the playground and they would rush out and separate the combatants and all would end in a handshake.

Sometimes, in the holidays and the glorious light evenings of summer, we would meet and play in Hylands Park. An abiding memory of those days is looking west down the hill towards Romford watching the sunset and listening to the trains and the clanking of the railway trucks in the marshalling yard by Romford Railway Station. The only fly in the ointment at Hylands Park was 'Parky,' or the park keeper. He wore a uniform with a peaked cap and his job was to make sure that we did not run on the flowerbeds or rub candle grease on the slide to give a faster ride! So long as we kept 'Parky' happy, life was uncomplicated.

David Clark

Two

Earning a Living

A Working Life

My father was a member of a firm of stockbrokers in Throgmorton Street in the City and wore the traditional suit, bowler hat and brolly. In the 1930s I was at a fee-paying college in Ilford to enable me to follow in his footsteps and enter the commercial life. My Uncle Stan was a stockbroker, Uncle Herman was manager of the Great Eastern Widows' & Orphans' Fund and Uncle Gordon was the accountant to the Nizam of Hyderabad Railway Co.

Father had volunteered for the Special Constabulary during the 1938 Munich crisis when we had to see pictures of that gullible man, Neville Chamberlain, waving his bit of paper around. On 3 September 1939 war was declared and father had to join the constabulary with a hefty reduction in income; therefore, I was to seek employment to help out with the family finances.

I promptly found work as office dogsbody at Hall & Co. Builders & Coal Merchants in Main Road, Romford, and there I learned the hard knocks of life and how to deal with all manner of people, customers, staff, lorry drivers and coalmen. My first job was to add up about 100 grimy sheets of vehicle's mileage, fuel consumption, hours worked late, so figure work became easy. I was seconded to a lovely man called Arthur Garwood who was manager of the Coal Delivery Dept. He smoked a pipe packed with St Bruno tobacco and wore an old, brown-tweed suit that almost fell to bits on him. My job was to answer the telephone, take coal orders, write out delivery tickets on what was called an Egry machine, prepare the journeys economically, as most deliveries were made by horse and cart, then make out delivery tickets for the yard foreman. I was a great favourite with the coalmen as I planned their journeys well and sometimes allowed them time to get an extra delivery in – hence a larger wage packet for the coalmen!

My first pay packet was 7s 6d, less HAS 4d and on the first Saturday after pay day, gave 2s 6d to my mother, went to the cinema for 1s, bought a pair of flannel trousers from a shop in South Street for 2s, rail fare Gidea Park to Romford for 1d and bought a 4oz slab of Bourneville chocolate for 4d and 'scoffed' the lot!

Each workday I went to the Hall & Co. yard to see what came in on the shunt. Puffing Billy came in daily with a load of coal trucks, there were Derby Brights, Normanton (the best fuel), kitchen nuts, anthracite from South Wales, and coke we picked up from Romford Gas Works. As the war progressed staff members were called up and more responsibility was put upon me. No time for instruction, you just got on with it. I moved to the building transport side of the business and much of our trade then was with Portland Cement collected from the CMC

Walter and Isabella Smith with their three eldest children, Oliver, Ruby and Ivy, 1904. Walter started the association with the brewery and four sons followed in his footsteps. (Sheila Acres)

Works at Grays and masses of sand and gravel. Many of our lorries were moved to Cambridge area for the construction of runways for the aerodromes springing up; those left in Romford coped with war damage repairs. I made up the wage packets from drivers' time sheets including those for the Cambridge area. A phone call to the National Provincial Bank in South Street for cash requirements, notes and coins, and my manager Dennis Peters took me in the Morris 8, then back again, to make up the wage packets behind locked doors and distribute. At times the yard foreman would take me to the Cambridge air sites to issue the money. A useful trip, for I made a beeline for the station NAAFI and loaded up with chocolate bars and Maltesers.

Chris Amis

A Family Affair

My grandfather, Walter Smith, was the first of our family to work at the brewery in Romford but not the last, as many more members of the Smith family were to follow in his footsteps. Walter Smith commenced his working career in the transport department at Ind Coope Brewery, Romford, during the First World War and continued to be employed there, even after he reached retirement age, as green keeper of the beautiful bowling green. This was part of the sports facilities available for employees within the brewery site. He took great pride

The Smith Family, 1947. Back row, left to right: Bert, Donald, Wally, Mick. Front row: Rhoda, Ivy, Ruby, Isabella and Walter Smith. (Sheila Acres)

in keeping everything pristine and enjoyed the many compliments he received on the high standard of his work there. My uncle, Oliver Smith, grandad's eldest son, followed him into the brewery to earn a living and later was followed by two more sons, my Uncles Walter and Donald. The youngest son, Uncle Bert, also followed on and continued this family tradition, also working in the transport area. Wally was in the cooperage area at the brewery and one of a breed known as a 'sniffer', his job being to 'sniff' the barrels prior to the filling with beer. If they found the smell was 'sour' the barrel would be rejected. Wally had a son, Derek, known as Mick, who also worked for the brewery in the transport section like his grandad. Teddy Saggers, a son-in-law, in contrast worked at the water works. None of grandad's three daughters were actually employed at the brewery but each showed a keen interest in the company. When one of your family members was involved at the brewery it became a family affair for there were aspects of the company facilities and celebrations which embraced family members. All good planning for the relationships with the workforce and gaining respect for the company as a good employer in the town. My grandmother Isabella and grandfather Walter Smith lived in the brewery cottages in Waterloo Road when that road was full of terrace cottages. They lived there very happily opposite the brewery workplace until the 1960s when the cottages were demolished to make way for the high-rise flats and assorted housing which stand on the site today and is known as the Waterloo Road Estate. Grandad Walter began a family tradition when he started work at the brewery. Throughout their working life in Romford, the Smith family boasted that grandad was the first employee followed by his four sons and then a further generation of three grandsons. All proud to be known as Romford Brewery Boys!

Sheila Acres (*née*) Sallows

The Brewery sports ground with bowling green within the brewery yard. (Sheila Acres)

At the Ind Coope reception area in the High Street, these young ladies would receive and direct all visitors to the brewery, 1990. Left to right: Karen and Lisa standing, Pamela Grieve and Sandra Meekings seated. (Pamela Grieve)

The Brewery

I well remember the Romford Brewery belching out fumes into the surrounding streets and all over the town it seemed when they were brewing. Some said they liked the smell but most did not. But this was the place of my husband's final job as a member of the security staff. He joined the company after leaving the army and continued there until he retired. We both went on a week-long pre-retirement course at Wansfell College, Theydon Bois, organised by the brewery for those approaching retirement. We joined the Brewery Pensioners' Club, which used to be held in the Brewery Sports & Social Club Hall, and Phil eventually became chairman and I secretary of a very successful weekly gathering until his death in 1990. A bench seat dedicated to his memory is positioned nearby the brewery gate in High Street funded by a collection of club members at that time. I still act as secretary at the club, now held at St Andrew's Parish Hall, although many of the 'old timers' are no longer with us. It has been a long association with Romford over the years, but it is no longer the town I knew as a child – the carefree days and the freedom to roam and play that I enjoyed is no longer possible for the children of today.

Judy Smith (*née*) Watters

A Policeman's Lot

My father was a CID detective sergeant at Romford during the war, in a reserved occupation, frustrated that he could not join up, as he came from a military family. However, he had a lively war on the home front. He was involved in tracking down deserters, black marketers and caught at least one spy. He got a commendation for stopping a panic-stricken crowd trying to get out of an air-raid shelter during an air raid. They would have poured straight out into an inferno. He jammed himself in the doorway. He was built like a barn door anyway! My mother was annoyed because the fire not only singed his hair, it burnt the back of his overcoat, which was a write-off! However, after the war, he was offered a commission as a major with the British Control Commission in Germany reconstructing the West German Police.

Deserters were sometimes armed with revolvers or automatics, which they had stolen. My father and other officers chased one armed deserter and cornered him on the roof of Sainsbury's in South Street. My father rushed forward and managed to disarm him before he could get a shot off. The spy was an Irish woman who frequented the dances held at RAF Hornchurch. She always asked the Canadian pilots about the armament and performance of their fighters, which towards the end of the war were Spitfires. She was arrested and handed over to the military. I often wonder what became of her. Policing did have a lighter side, however. The Canadian airmen had a great capacity for drink and scant respect for our licensing laws. One night in 1944, six had been drinking in the Lamb in Romford Market and were refusing to leave after hours, demanding more drink. Dad was called to get them to leave, but they decided to beat him up. An unwise move on their part, as Dad took them all on and knocked all six unconscious! He then had the problem of getting them to the police station in South Street. He hailed a passing cyclist and commandeered his bicycle. Then both Dad and the cyclist put them one at a time over the handlebars and wheeled them to the police station. He told us this story over breakfast next morning with two black eyes, bruised knuckles and a big grin!

Romford was in the Essex Constabulary and the dividing line between its area and the Metropolitan Police crossed the London Road between Romford and Chadwell Heath. There were plenty of drunks about on a Saturday night. Some were incapable, which meant that the police had to arrest them and put them into cells. Sometimes the Romford Police, to save trouble, would take the incapable ones up the London Road and dump them over the border where they became the responsibility of the Met. The Met, of course, would do the same from their side. Many a drunk has spent the night being transported unconscious backwards and forwards over the border! Dad left Romford in 1949, but when he retired in 1959, he still held the record for the most arrests in one year in Romford, which was 206, and he had earned the nickname 'Fearless Fred.'

David Clark

A Sainsbury Butter Patter

My husband came from a family of farmers in the village of Lambourne End, Essex, the youngest son of a family of ten children. His name was Philip and I was Phyllis and we were known to all as the two 'Phils.' After we married we came to live in Essex Road and the house was a rebuild on a bombsite, a clearance plot caused by the terrible raid in which many lost their lives in 1941. I worked at the Sainsbury shop in South Street where the walls were lined with pristine tiles. The staff were required to take a turn at all the counters so I served my time on the grocery and provisions section, cooked meats and dairy foods, including the well-remembered time as a 'butter patter.' From a great lump of butter could be taken the required amount and patted into a convenient shape with wooden 'patters' and a neat square then wrapped for the customer in a greaseproof paper. I eventually became a senior leading sales person. Around 1950 I moved on to Grant Barnett who were umbrella manufacturers and stayed with them for around seven years. My husband by this time was working with Grants of St James, a wine and spirit company operating within the brewery yard at Romford. He later transferred to Ind Coope Brewery and worked in the stores department of the transport section. Now a widow, I have happy memories of Romford and still attend the old Brewery Pensioners' Club although most of the old friends are gone now and only a few remain.

We did not have children of our own so were able to enjoy much travel together from say 1957. I now mull over my memories of our travels together from happy times in the West Country at home, then abroad in France, all over west and eastern Europe, and as travelling abroad became available to the masses we progressed even further, with travels to America, Canada and Hawaii. So although I have lived a great many years in Romford, in the same house in Essex Road, I have indeed looked over the horizon and seen much of the world but I hasten to add, I have always been glad to return to my hometown of Romford.

Phyllis Threader

Pin Money

Like many young teens in the 1950s while still at Romford County High School I obtained employment to earn some pin money and I remember working at Christmas time in a photographers in Victoria Road to supplement my requirements for Christmas spending money and all was fine. Another time I worked in a toyshop in the High Street. It was near the brewery and almost opposite F.W. Woolworth; the building was a tall, Victorian shop with creaky wooden floorboards and a groaning wooden staircase which led to the storage rooms above. I never liked to go to the storeroom, so dismal, dim and dusty, and when I made the scary

Marks & Spencer staff, 1930s. (Lesley Godbold)

assent I would wonder why I stayed. I really did not like it up there and I was so scared – and all for 10s a day! I wonder if anyone remembers buying toys for their children there, unaware of course of how uneasy I felt if anything was needed from the storeroom. Several years later and still determined to make a little money, I started a little business of my own, making the fashionable 'can-can' petticoats, a 'must have' item of clothing for young girls at the time. I also made fancy aprons or pinnies as there were sometimes called, all to my own individual designs. I always bought my materials in the Romford Arcade for the shops supplied fabrics of all kinds, a wonderland for a dressmaker. Masses of materials were available and my requirements were available for the princely sum of 2s 6p per yard!

Jean Pound (*née*) Williams

My Mother's Shop

During my early teenage years my mother bought a grocery store within a small terraced house in Laurel Crescent, Rush Green; it was situated in the front room of the house and we lived at the back of the building. There was a conservatory, which served as a stock room. We did not have a proper shop window but the original house window served the purpose for displaying goods with an advertising poster above. This little venture proved to be fairly successful and served the purpose well in providing an income. I remember one night there was a particular incident that was unexpected and a nasty surprise. There was a false ceiling in the hall in which were housed the cigarettes, sweets and the R. Whites fizzy drinks which were stored in wooden crates in the hall. This particular hot summer night a bottle of cherryade exploded – the noise

Mrs Theresa Baker with her daughter Pauline at the grocery store at Laurel Close, Rush Green. (Pauline Hollingsworth)

was bad enough, but there was also glass and sticky fluid everywhere. It took simply ages to clear the mess and not everything could be saved. But apart from this kind of little mishap I think mother enjoyed her little venture into the world of commerce!

Pauline Hollingsworth (*née*) Baker

Working Life in Romford

After National Service, I returned to Romford and went back to Peter Grahams, a local firm of manufacturing opticians and was promptly offered a promotion to a position as representative salesman covering the south coast of England. Being a representative was all very well, but I missed the opportunity to socialise with friends at home. One particular weekend at home, I met an old friend who I had known since my primary school days and he told me that he was working at the local brewery and he found it a very good firm to work for. As I was interested in local work he recommended me for an interview and subsequently I joined the work force in 1961 and remained there for the next thirty years, mostly employed within the quality control area of the laboratory. Now retired, I look back on those years at the brewery with appreciation for the great opportunities available and the good crowd of colleagues around me. I shall always be grateful for that good advice from a childhood friend. When I was established in my working career, I married my wife, Annette, in 1966 and although we now enjoy retirement in Woodbridge, Suffolk, we both remember our Romford days with affection.

Ron Fuller

A date at the Kursal, Southend, 1950s. Del Osborne and wife Sheila now live in Melbourne, Australia. (Del Osborne)

Ring-road developments to come, here we see Mercury House and the Dolphin Leisure Centre still standing at the right-hand side of picture with the distinctive pyramid-shaped roof. (Patrick Arnold)

Going 'Down Under'

I well remember my first job when I left school aged fourteen – it was at the Maypole Dairy Co. in South Street. Burton's the tailors was next door and the Home & Colonial Store was next to that. From there I progressed in my working life until aged eighteen it was time for National Service, my call up papers arrived and I ended up serving in Germany with the British occupational forces. I was with the British Army of the Rhine from 1950 to 1952. I married in 1963, Sheila Pendley, a local girl from Harold Hill; she had worked at the Gaumont Cinema. In 1964, we decided to try our luck on the other side of the world and investigated our chances at Australia House. We decided to emigrate to Australia, a big move but one we do not regret. Like so many others we have brought up our three children here, they have married and we now have seven grandchildren holding us very strongly to our adopted land. But memories of our former 'home' and of our young days are still with us and we have been lucky enough to revisit from time to time. But how Romford has changed: we got lost on the one-way systems and the streets I had known in the past which had led to the Market Place were now cut off. We looked for the Gaumont Cinema where Sheila had worked but it had disappeared! The shops that I knew in South Street when I worked at the dairy were mostly all gone. We intend to come back at least one more time to see how many more changes have taken place. Well that's progress they say, changing needs and changing times.

We are retired now and live in a retirement village, which works for us; there is so much available for the community, and we like to take on our share of the organisation. Residents are able to take part in a varied social life here and enjoy a sense of belonging to a community that cares.

Derek (Del) Osborne

Model Girls

I have many happy memories of Romford from my childhood in the 1950s, when I would go with Dad to the Market Place when the animals were still in their pens. Dad would buy what were called 'day old chicks' to take home to rear; the chicks were sold in big cardboard boxes with little holes in them giving them air while journeying home. Later on when I was a teenager I was thrilled when my first try at a modelling career started to take off and it all began in Romford. Along with others, I started modelling wedding dresses for Hanburys in the High Street – in the 1960s it was the place to go to buy or hire your wedding dress! We were commissioned by Hanbury to model the latest styles in bridal wear and this was considered a new innovation at the time. It was all such fun, we made quite a splash in the High Street, usually six young models all dressed in wedding finery would pile into a large van, many clad in the fashionable 'meringue' bridal wear so popular in that period and then we sped off for our 'shoot' locations. Our dressers and photographers following on, we went to various country houses in the area, such as the Ford owned Bower House at Havering-atte-Bower. The photographs were used all over Britain and led to other modelling work, particularly in swimsuits, so I worked for Slix and Nelbarden, both famous swimsuit manufacturers. My pictures also graced the pages of 'do-it-yourself', home magazines, and included work for the local Hendersen Sliding Door Factory. Eventually modelling held less attraction and other skills and training superseded my modelling days. However to have that experience as a very young girl was something I would have been sorry to miss.

Sylvia Kent (*née*) Bray

Hanbury Bridal Wear models off for a 'shoot' on location at country houses, 1950s. (Sylvia Kent)

A Dog's Life

Life in the police force was the life for me and I greatly enjoyed a successful career for many years. This is an amusing tale from my early Romford days.

In 1958 Romford and surrounding areas were part of the largest police division in the Essex County Constabulary including the new and large council estate of Harold Hill. This area adjoined East London districts and attracted criminal elements from London and as a result the division boasted the largest CID unit, with a detective chief inspector as the divisional CID commander. He had a fine reputation with a good record behind him and had enjoyed a fine public image in the local and national newspapers. When on annual leave his deputy was eager to cope in a way to emulate his boss. This particular day I was trying to catch up with a mountain of paper work for we had no typists or word processors in those days. He called me to accompany him to a household where a child had gone missing and other officers were to meet us there having alerted the press to the incident. The child had last been seen in a field at the end of the garden, a search party was organised and two reporters from the local press were there. One uniformed officer jumped to attention and informed the boss that 'the dog' had been sent for. The dog referred to was the sole member of the newly formed Essex Police Dog Unit, only a week in existence and formed of a trained Alsatian from the Surrey Police and an ex-RAF handler, a new aid for the Essex officers. The rules declared the dog was to be called to all incidents involving missing children, so we awaited the arrival of dog and handler. On arrival the dog handler was resplendent in his new uniform complete with blue jodhpurs and highly polished leather gaiters and called his magnificent dog to his side. The air was filled with expectation. The assembled officers and general public around and about or leaning from upstairs windows waited in anticipation. The dog handler, the star attraction, smartly marched to the end of the garden and gave a faultless salute enquiring if he should commence the dog tracking, still noting all eyes were upon him. The detective inspector had no time for this new fangled police assistance and watched exasperated as the dog refused for the third time an invitation to jump the fence into the field. Even when the handler went over the fence and called him, the dog merely put his paws on the fence and started barking. The detective inspector had now become outraged at the performance, much to the amusement of the swelled crowd of about 100 onlookers. With real embarrassment the handler jumped back into the garden and threw the dog into the field. The dog recovered and leapt back into the garden, bounded over to the detective inspector and promptly relieved itself with cocked leg over his trouser leg! The gathered assembly howled with laughter, but the boss just stood speechless. Then a young police constable appeared reporting the search had been called off: the child had been found playing in her friend's coal shed. The incident did receive press attention that week but it was not the kind of publicity that had been hoped for. Since those early days, the Essex Police Dog Section has progressed to become one of the most efficient, well–trained and best–equipped units in the United Kingdom.

Derek Wyatt

A Family Firm

There must be many Romford people who will remember 'Pollards', a household name when it came to everyday family needs in clothes and household linens, but few would know that the business started well over 100 years ago in the area now known as Docklands. My grandfather,

Typical Pollard's shop window display. (Kathleen Pollard)

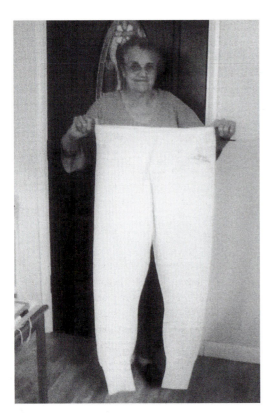

Famous for underwear and a favourite
for long johns, this pair still preserved
from stock. Label reads 'All wool – shrink
resisting'. (Kathleen Pollard)

who started the business, came from Yorkshire and his father, my great-grandfather, was also listed as a linen draper in the same county. In 1892 grandfather was operating a similar business in Canning Town and continued there until 1903. My father was born in 1900 and followed the family tradition of working in the business, which expanded successfully, buying and selling all kinds of wares, which at one time included a consignment of chamber pots, ex-sample goods carried to the customer by representatives to obtain orders for complete washing sets, a washing set being a popular household item at the time. The shops were able to sell these chamber pots priced 6d or a 'tanner', and as late as 1945 customers were telling us they still had these items, but not necessarily in use! My father went into the Navy in 1917 during the First World War and was demobbed in 1919, then it was business as usual with his father and in 1922 the business became a limited company. My mother and father married in 1923 and mother also worked in the shop. My father opened his own branch in 1931 by the Old Vic Theatre. His own ideas very much to the fore, he created the company slogan, 'Reliable Goods, Reasonably Priced, Honestly Sold.' In 1934 the business extended to Plaistow and my brother and I, were of an age to be of some help in the shop. The prices I remember most were those ending in 'three farthings' and the practice was to offer a small item of haberdashery to cover the farthing change!

By 1940 we had extended to East Ham and then continued to acquire one or two shops each year, including the first branch in Havering, the Elm Park branch in 1948, followed by Hornchurch in 1950, Collier Row in 1954 and later Harold Hill and Romford. By 1957 there were twenty-seven branches operating and by 1966 a further eight branches in south and east London. There were sixty-eight Pollard shops within the Greater London area, Herts and Essex. New staff were often recruited from relations of staff already working for us or the grown–up children or grandchildren of former staff members. A policy of recruitment which paid dividends, creating long–term relationships within the families, providing a staff with the tradition of working for Pollards, almost as strong as our own family commitment. Truly a family business until the end and the shops provided the standard of wares that were so valued by our loyal customers. Whenever we opened new stores we always seemed to find the reputation of the shop was already well known, for the previous generation had used the shops for supplies in the past. There were some products still popular with the older generation such as 'long john' underpants for men, and their women folk found the Pollard shops invaluable as a source for such items. Other goods, clothing and underwear for babies, children, ladies, through to grandparents were on offer. Every kind of household linen was displayed in our distinctive window displays, a system of shelving designed by my father was used to display a multitude of items in this way. Our popularity was emphasized by the manner of a body of loyal staff who demonstrated time and interest in serving the customer. An attitude sadly mostly lost to the shopper of today.

When father died in 1984 my brother was well equipped to continue with the family firm. I am retired now of course and still living in Havering, I have gathered the social history of our family firm together and am pleased to have these notes included in this book of memories. My own memories of being part of a family firm striving to bring goods to the customer in the tradition of our store slogan, 'Reliable Goods, Reasonably Priced, Honestly Sold', are accompanied with a sense of pride. From great grandfather through the generations, the world of drapery and haberdashery saw many changes. I witnessed the social history of this particular trade and enjoyed my experience with traders, colleagues, and customers. Our family ties run deep and continue to do so to this day.

Kathleen Pollard

The Brewery Chimney

The brewery chimney, which today is still one of the most significant reminders of the brewing industry's long association with the town of Romford, towers over the retail complex also known as 'the Brewery.' The former brewery, established in 1799, continued brewing until 1993, and was one of the foremost employers in the town. In 1965 a colleague, Mr Wilfred Willcox, an independent civil and structural engineer and myself, an independent quantity surveyor were appointed to oversee construction work in the brewery between 1965 and the 1980s. Dennis Jubb & Partners were structural engineers commissioned by Ind Coope Ltd to redevelop the brewery. As their office was in Bath, Somerset, they appointed Mr Willcox and myself to provide the professional services rendered on site. Mr Willcox designed the reinforced concrete chimney in 1966; it stood 150ft high and was built by Sir Robert McAlpine, contractors, at a cost of £15,000. It was built using a 'slip form' type of formwork into which reinforcement was placed and concrete poured. When set, the formwork was raised to the next section until the full height was reached. This was quite new technology in this country at that time. The chimney was raised in the late 1970s to avoid down draughts, which affected the performance of the boiler and at that time it was painted white and the name Romford Brewery was painted on the top sections of the raised chimney. Between 1965 and 1980, virtually all the major buildings within the brewery site were rebuilt to new designs and to suit the change in brewing methods being introduced into the industry. The works were carried out by three large construction companies, Sir Robert McAlpine, W. & C. French Ltd and John Laing Ltd.

The Ind Coope Brewery, formerly a foremost local industry, 1960s. (Michael Willcox)

A busy brewery yard, the chimney the only remaining item left today at 'the Brewery' shopping complex, 1960s. (Michael Willcox)

My part in these matters at that time are still well remembered and it is with good memories I recall this part of my professional career. The brewery chimney is a reminder to me of former associations and that this still stands as a symbol and a monument to the brewery years is gratifying. All these years later on a visit to London, an outing, which included a trip on the London Eye, with the day being clear and bright, the brewery chimney at Romford was clearly viewable from that distance!

Fred Shaw

Market Trader

Our family will celebrate seventy-five years of market trading in the town of Romford in 2008, which is a record the family is justly proud of. It all began in 1933 in a new shop in the Quadrant Arcade when it was first established in the town and later moved out into the Market Place proper. Charles Fancourt, my father, was not only renowned as a fine fishmonger in the town but also as a great sportsman, most famously for his years of dedication to Romford Bowls Club of which he was president. A supporter of sport in general he believed in the concept that it was a worthy training programme for life. The market stall continued to serve customers throughout the war years, Dad travelling to Billingsgate Market in some dangerous circumstances at times to obtain fish for the Romford stall. Later deliveries by train were organised from the east-coast fishing ports so that the business continued. My parents lived in Carlton Road during the 1940s and lived there through the war years when Romford experienced many bombing

At the fish stall in the market, left to right: Edward Fancourt (nephew), Charles Fancourt, Charles Fancourt (senior). (Edward Fancourt)

Celebrating a new venture. From left to right: Edward Fancourt, West Ham footballer Julian Dicks, nephew Charles. (Edward Fancourt)

raids, but happily they survived to welcome the victory celebrations thereafter. Following in the footsteps of my father I was attracted to the fish trade and worked with Dad at the market stall. In 1977 for the Silver Jubilee we had a special fish auction, which attracted large crowds and received a great deal of attention. There were many champagne cork-popping moments over the years, not least when Julian Dicks, the great West Ham footballing hero and legend on the field and a first-class player, came to the stall and opened the bubbly to celebrate a new start with my nephew, another Charles Fancourt, as we ran the stall together at that time. In 1997 the celebrations of the 750th anniversary of the Market Place brought an official week of celebrations to the town and a sense of history in being part of this trading community. It will be my privilege and pleasure to be still representing the name of Fancourt in the Market Place on our anniversary date in 2008.

Edward Fancourt

Three

Birth, Marriage and a Funeral

Birth to Laying Out

Mother was a young widow and I only two years old when father died of TB in 1923. Left with three daughters and two sons to bring up alone was not easy, so mother put her hand to many tasks to see that we had all we needed. Our mother undertook cleaning jobs outside the home and was regularly called upon to act as midwife and helper to look after families during the confinement period. Mother would monitor the stages of labour and call for help as required. Sometimes she made herself available for the whole of the 'lying in' period and looked after the cooking for the family and took care of any young children in the household. As well as this vital assistance occasionally she would be called upon to give the necessary attentions to the dead, which involved 'laying out' procedures. If people had need of assistance there was usually a local person who they could go to for such help and my mother was the person many turned to in these circumstances.

Ethel Whitehead (*née*) Shelley

Born in a Stable

When I lived in a shared household in the 1930s at the top of the Market Place, the owner of the big house had called the midwife to her married daughter who suddenly had gone into labour while she was visiting the stables at the rear of the property. The wait seemed interminable as we all kept watching for the midwife. The baby, however, would not delay entry into this world and nature took its course. The baby was born in the stable at the bottom of the garden not far away from 'Bess' the horse. When the midwife finally arrived to inspect the situation she was not best pleased and remarked, that in all her experience she had never known such a thing. The smiling and happy grandmother replied, 'Well you have now!'

Muriel Arnold (*née*) Lilley

The Midwife

I continue to this day in the nursing profession and have always enjoyed my work, for the satisfaction it has given me and the many and varied contacts it has allowed me in my career.

Len and Jose Hollingsworth celebrate a war-time marriage at Eastern Road Registry Office, 1943. (Jose Hollingsworth)

The years I worked as a community midwife in Havering, which embraced Romford of course, are still fresh in my mind and include many happy memories. When I arrived on the scene for an expected delivery, you can imagine how people welcomed me with open arms. The relief on many a father's face, had to be seen to be believed! Also the anticipation on the faces of older siblings often entrenched on the stairs awaiting the new arrival. I have always considered it a great privilege to witness the arrival of thousands of babies into this world and play my part in the safe delivery of a newborn and share the joy with the parents. My work took me into every kind of home and all types of situations but whatever the circumstances, my job was to deal with mother and baby in a professional way.

Adelaide Hikel (née) McAllister

Blue Sapphire Anniversary

What a celebration when we marked our sixty-five years of marriage on 22 January 2008 with family and friends around us, proudly displaying our card from the Queen, for our blue-sapphire anniversary. As with most wartime weddings, my husband wore his uniform of the Kings Royal Rifle Co., the 9th Armoured Division. Due to an accident affecting his hand he was deemed unable to work with a rifle and therefore became an army driver mainly serving in Northern Ireland during the war. We were married in 1943 at the register office, which at that time was in Eastern Road, Romford. We moved into the house in Carlton Road with my mother-in-law, where my husband and I still live. We met in Silverstone, Northamptonshire, my home ground, when he was working as an army driver and I was training to be a teacher. It was a wartime romance that would not be denied so we married and I stayed with his mother in Romford while he continued his army service. When later I became pregnant, Romford was being bombed frequently. I returned to my roots and went home to mother in Silverstone where our two boys were born. The first-born was premature and my husband was allowed home on compassionate leave and was relieved to see that mother and baby had survived the ordeal of a difficult birth. After the war we were reunited and returned to Carlton Road and continued to live with my mother-in-law until her death in 1970. My husband was a fully trained baker and pastry cook and post-war returned to his trade working at various Romford bakers. He had a very successful career at the Co-operative Bakers and with the locally famous Speights Bakery. He produced wonderful celebration cakes for most of the 'highlight' events of our family life, together with a fantastic array of pastries for our table. Our splendid celebrations this year, a 'surprise' affair at our son and daughter-in-law's home in Chelmsford, included three generations of our family, our two sons with their wives, four grandchildren and three great grandchildren. It was lovely to have them all about us at such a happy time and we reminisced about the past and the changes we had witnessed since those wartime days long ago. Little did we know when we started out, what a long and happy marriage would lay before us. We have always been content with our home in Carlton Road, Romford, which has been home to my husband for well over seventy years.

Joscelyne Hollingsworth (*née*) Denney

Coming to Collier Row

I met my husband, a builder, in 1928 when I lived at Grass Farm, Wallasea Island, and we married at Rawreth in 1930. We moved to Collier Row, Romford, for my husband to work on the new houses being built in Lowshoe Lane. Mr Martin, father of Millicent Martin, famous for the satirical programme *That was the Week that Was*, was the developer. We rented rooms in the big house called Elmhurst. Our two rooms were rented for the princely sum of 5s a week. The freeholder was Mr Bertram Nicholls and his wife looked after the rental affairs. The stables were let to a riding school and some outbuildings were rented by Mr Leggett, who kept greyhounds there and this was the man who later developed the Romford Stadium Greyhound Track in London Road. There were difficult times in the 1930s with many unemployed and the 'hungry thirties' were beginning to bite and the need for soup kitchens saw Elmhurst completely convert a stable for that purpose. The stable was organised with gas rings for heating the soup and people came with basins to be served. My landlady organised the whole matter and I think the council provided the money to purchase the ingredients. About 1937 Elmhurst was sold, with the exception of two cottages opposite the Bell and Gate public house site, also now demolished. New Ideal Homesteads demolished Elmhurst to build the Elmhurst Park Estate. We happily survived these lean years at the start of our married life and made Romford our home. As time eased the financial strain and things were improving, my husband, who had always been keen on motorbikes, purchased a Velocette and I have fond memories of our travels together all over the county of Essex and beyond, and we continued to travel in tandem throughout our married life.

Muriel Arnold (*née*) Lilley

Fear of Flying

I was born in Collier Row in 1921 and married later than the average bride. I married in 1954 at the register office located in Eastern Road at that time. Our happy marriage lasted for twenty-five years until my husband died in 1979. He had owned Whitehead's grocery stores at Collier Row and originally following our wedding we lived over the shop in a first-floor flat which was part of the premises. Later we moved to Main Road, Gidea Park, and finally to my present home. We did not have any children but very much enjoyed our life together and the opportunity to travel on many holidays both at home and abroad. We travelled extensively by road and rail and sea yet I have never flown in an aeroplane, preferring to travel by any other mode of travel, by car and coach and channel ferries, which gave us a gateway to Europe and beyond. My mother had come to live with us when I was nursing my husband in his final illness and was there with me when he died. This company, beneficial for both of us, was short lived as mother died soon after and I have lived alone since that very sad time. Fortunately I have a number of nieces and nephews and good neighbours to help with my shopping needs and I walk to the local shops and the post office for exercise and to obtain the rest of my few requirements. I have enjoyed my life in and around the town of Romford and have few regrets looking back over the years.

Ethel Whitehead (*née*) Shelley

On the Carpet

When my grandparents, Walter and Isabella Smith, dressed in wedding guest finery, they had a photograph taken in the back garden. In this precious picture they can be seen standing on a piece of carpet to save soiling their best shoes. Years later, on the occasion of my own wedding

Walter Smith and Isabella in rear garden standing on a piece of carpet to protect their footwear, 1920s. (Sheila Acres)

Sheila Sallow's wedding day. Although Grandad Walter Smith was too frail to attend the church this photograph was taken at his side as he wished her happiness on the way to St Andrew's Church. (Sheila Acres)

at St Andrew's Church, grandad was not well enough to come to the church for the ceremony, but as I prepared to leave the family home he stood beside me to wish me well and to see me on my way. I treasure the photograph taken together as I left for the church.

Sheila Acres (*née*) Sallows

Perfect October Day

On 8 October 1955 the sun shone brightly on our wedding day and the marriage took place at Romford Register Office in Brentwood Road. I had known Peter, my husband to be, for a long time as my sister, Molly, was married to his brother, Mac. However, we had only been going out together for eighteen months when I accepted his proposal of marriage. The bride did not usually wear a white bridal gown at a register office wedding in those days and my fashionable choice of dress on the day was a dark-green fabric with white flock dots on it, I had been told that to wear the colour green was unlucky, but as the marriage has lasted fifty-two years so far, I dismiss this as a nonsense. I still have that dress today. My accessories were a little white hat together with peep-toe shoes and clutch handbag to match and a corsage of rosebuds on my dress. My husband, Peter, suited and booted and wearing a white carnation in his lapel buttonhole, looked my ideal husband. All went well at the ceremony and we returned to my parents' home, where my mother had worked hard putting together a lovely reception. A houseful of guests joined us for a really good time and it was a perfect day for us. When we left the reception it was in some style, my friend Jean and her American fiancé drove us away in

Hilda Wilson and Peter Bennett married at the Brentwood Road Register Office, 1955. (Hilda Bennett)

Hilda and Peter Bennett took off from Southend Airport on the honeymoon special with other newly weds, destination Jersey, Channel Islands, 1955. (Hilda Bennett)

his 'posh' American car to Southend airport where we were to go on board the 'Honeymoon Special' flight, our destination Jersey, in the Channel Isles. This was a number one choice for a honeymoon at the time and we met up with a party of three other newly wedded couples for the flight. The plane had twelve seats and we all started our married lives seated and ready on board as the engines came to life, we were lifted up on the wind where we experienced some bumping and bouncing as we took off on our very first flight! Very glad to report that in the years that followed 'turbulence' was very limited.

Hilda Bennett (*née*) Wilson

A Story from Adelaide

St Edward's Roman Catholic Church is another important church available to the people of Romford. It was here in 1955 that my aunt Maureen Brightwell married my Uncle Jack McGavin. After their marriage, they lived locally and raised their two children, a girl and a boy, here and things progressed well enough. Then a great deal of publicity of great chances in Australia and a recruitment campaign running for what was known as the '£10 Pom' scheme. This offered subsisted passage to a new land for those accepted, in return for an undertaking to remain there for a minimum period of two years. The appeal of this idea attracted an application from the couple when they began thinking of making a step into the unknown. Arriving in Adelaide, South Australia, in May 1964 with their two children, Gillian, aged six, and Stewart, almost four, the adventure began. When they arrived in Adelaide they were in temporary housing for two months until the brand new house they had bought in Salisbury, South

St Edward's Roman Catholic Church, Park End Road, Romford, Essex. (Chris Amis)

Maureen and Jack McGavin married at the Roman Catholic Church in Romford, 1955. Today they live in Adelaide, South Australia, after emigrating with their children in 1964. (Pauline Hollingsworth)

Australia, was completed; a house in which they still live forty-four years on. Jack got a job in the administration department of the Highways Department, later moving to weapons research and finally ending up in the budgeting department of the University of South Australia, where he stayed until he retired. He also became a Justice of the Peace. Maureen was a 'stay at home' mother until the children were older and, at the age of forty, started working as a pharmacy assistant in the local chemist, a post she held for twenty-two years. The children both did well, one becoming a radiographer and the other owning her own business and finally ending up in the local radio station. The children both married and have children of their own, who are all doing well in their chosen careers. So a marriage, which started out here in Romford, has succeeded 'down under' because a young family put their best foot forward and made the most of a fine opportunity.

Pauline Hollingsworth (*née*) Baker

Oh, Happy Day

There could not have been a more appropriate church for my wedding day than that of St Edward the Confessor, which stands in the Market Place at Romford. For I was to marry into a family of long-term market traders and as my wedding day dawned and I dressed in my bridal finery I knew the day would be a happy one. Most importantly, I knew my handsome husband was the right one for me. All the thought and planning was over and I was content with my two older bridesmaids in their beautiful gowns, neat headdresses and floral bouquets, the two

Joyce and Charles Fancourt, junior, married at St Edward's Church in the Market Place. (Joyce Fancourt)

Joyce and Charles Fancourt, junior, at the church in the Market Place with the many guests. (Joyce Fancourt)

young pageboys rigged out with smart suits and Eton collars complete with bow ties, and to complete the picture the tiny bridesmaids looking sweet and lovely. All the guests were awaiting my entrance and the walk down the aisle went without mishap. The vows expressed, the register signed, we emerged from the church and into the sunshine together to be greeted by a vast army of guests all in their wedding outfits with hats aplenty for the ladies and flocked nylon fabric in abundance, which was most fashionable at the time. Family and friends surrounding us, good wishes were coming from all sides, we settled down for the photographs and followed the photographers instruction to say 'cheese' so it was big smiles all round. They say that every girl dreams of her wedding day and should feel like a princess on her big day and I just want to say here that was certainly true for me the day I married in Romford Market Place over fifty years ago.

Joyce Fancourt (née) Perfect

Fateful Harvest Festival

When I left Romford County High School, I, like many others, started my working life commuting to the great City of London, but my social life was mainly on home territory. I met my future husband at a Harvest festival supper in Hornchurch and my fate was sealed. Fifteen months later we were married at the Romford Register Office in Brentwood Road. Romford played a part in my wedding preparations for I bought my wedding dress in the

Jean and Sam Pound married at the Brentwood Road Register Office, 1955. (Jean Pound)

Happy group photograph of some wedding guests at the wedding of Jean and Sam. Jean's younger sister Valerie Williams is bridesmaid. (Jean Pound)

Market Place, pale blue with a quilted panel down the front, a snip at £2 10s. My dark blue 'duster coat' I bought at Frances Dee in South Street, a little pale blue feathery hat, 'strappy' toeless sling-back high heels, and a corsage of carnations and tiny rosebuds completed my ensemble. At that time, the early 1950s, the register office venue, a Victorian villa, old and dark inside, did not particularly impress; there were battered hard dining chairs in the hallway and bridal nerves were at their height at this stage before the ceremony. However, there was a much brighter marriage room and flower arrangements completed the ambiance making a much more welcoming place for the taking of our vows. When the proceedings commenced, I was surprised to find a lady registrar in charge of events, but was without time to even think about this for more than a moment. As we proceeded I was so nervous, I did a Princess Diana and got my husband's names mixed up and, full of confusion, pronounced his Christian names back to front! My husband was in the meat trade and at one time worked in the Romford Arcade for Sheward's the butchers – he progressed from those early days to establishing his own wholesale meat company.

I had a successful career teaching in Essex and it was years later after my retirement that I returned to Romford to see how the place had changed. The changes were many, I could not recognise many of the areas I had known and as for going into Romford by car, I would be hopelessly lost! We have moved to new areas of Essex several times during our fifty-three years of marriage and now live in Clacton-on-Sea. I am an Essex girl and proud to be so and as far as I am concerned Essex still reaches to the River Lee!

Jean Pound (*née*) Williams

Ellen and Graham Preston married in the Market Place church of St Edward just as Ellen had always planned. It was a market day and the shoppers stopped to wish her well. (Ellen Preston)

After their wedding, Ellen and Graham Preston walking in the grounds of St Edward's Church. The photograph shows the attraction of this lovely place in the heart of Romford. (Ellen Preston)

St Edward's Market Place Church

I dreamed of marrying in St Edward's Church in the Market Place at Romford, and on 2 August 1975 on a Saturday and thus a market day – my wish came true. All the stalls were out and great crowds would stop shopping to watch a bridal party arrive and wish the bride good luck on her special day. This was my special day and I stood with my father outside the church on arrival. I remember how proud he was while photographs were taken of us together before he led me into the church for the service and to play his part in giving me away to Graham, my husband to be. After the ceremony, we enjoyed the photographic session and as we left amid the cheering and good wishes it was a joyful occasion. Initially, we lived off Mawney Road in our first married home and enjoyed happy times in Romford. We have now been married for thirty-two years and have two grown-up children, a girl and a boy. Life has been good and we have travelled extensively over the years, but that church in the Market Place was where it all began for us!

Ellen Preston (née</em) Huggett

St Andrew's Church, Romford

My grandparents and my parents, Alfred and Marjorie Gage, had married at St Andrew's Church, Romford; my parents on 3 June 1939, that fateful year when by 3 September 1939 we were at

St Andrew's Church, St Andrew's Road, June 1939. Left to right: Amy Gage (mother of the bridegroom), bridesmaid ?, Ernest Gage (father of groom), Alfred Gage (groom), Ron Gage (brother and best man), Marjorie Gage (bride), guest, Rene Thorogood (sister of the bride), Herbert Thorogood (father of the bride). (Lesley Godbold)

A family tradition continued when Lesley Gage married her husband Steve at St Andrew's Church – her grandparents and parents had both married there. This interior shot shows the high altar at their ceremony. (Lesley Godbold)

war with Germany. They reached their golden wedding in 1989 and their diamond wedding in 1999. What a record! Therefore, on the occasion of my own wedding day there was no question that St Andrew's would be the venue for our own ceremony. I married my husband, Steve, in that lovely church and the large congregation of well wishes who witnessed the ceremony gave us their support, in this, one of the most important decisions we make in life. We were fortunate in having a photograph taken from the choir gallery on the day and the main altar is seen and it is interesting to note the various fashions worn by those present. Yet another wedding day recorded for my family and if we follow in the footsteps of my mother and father and manage to enjoy as many wedding anniversaries as they did, we will be most grateful.

Lesley Godbold (*née*) Gage

St Michael & All Saints Church

In this book you will see the story of the marriage of my in-laws, Mr and Mrs Hollingsworth, who celebrated sixty-five years of marriage in 2008. Len and Jose, as she is known, have achieved a blue-sapphire anniversary which we were pleased to celebrate with them. My own wedding to their son Tony, took place at the church of St Michael & All Saints Church, Gidea Park, on 22 December 1968. Although so near to Christmas, the photographs show a sparkling bright day outside the church. Much thought had gone into the design of my gown in the event of a freezing day and there was a coat-like design in the dress I wore, which I had made myself. Being a very practical person, I had also made my bridesmaid's gown and with flowers in our hair and pretty bouquets I was pleased with the results. Tony, my bridegroom,

A December wedding at Gidea Park was the choice of Pauline and Tony Hollingsworth when they married at St Michael & All Saints Church, and the wedding party stood in bright sunshine for a happy wedding-day picture. (Pauline Hollingsworth)

Farewell to a fishmonger. Mr Charles Fancourt took his final journey from the Market Place on 30 July 2003. He had sold fish in the market for more than seventy years. (Reprinted courtesy of the *Romford Recorder*)

looked a picture, sporting a fashionable beard of the time, his parents and brother in attendance and my mother and stepfather stood outside the church while the photographer recorded the event after the ceremony. My father-in-law was a master cake maker and was skilled in cake decoration, therefore the cake he produced was rather special. I was determined this wedding would be a memory for us that would be very lovely indeed, and so it was, but we were equally determined that it was even more important for us to devote most of our money towards a home of our own. We had bought our own property prior to the big day and this helped to get our priorities in order, and to this day forty years later we have never regretted that decision.

Pauline Hollingsworth (*née*) Baker

Funeral of the Godfather

My father, Charles Fancourt, fishmonger, was widely known as the Godfather of Romford Market as he and his family had sold fish there for over seventy years and his was a very well-known face among the market traders. When he died, aged ninety-three, the Market Place was witness to the significant and solemn occasion of his funeral, which took place at the Market Place church of St Edward the Confessor in August 2003. Dad had worked in the shadow of that church for so long during his working life and had very much enjoyed his years associated with the market. A horse-drawn, glass-sided hearse arrived at the church for the service, on top of which was displayed an appropriate floral tribute shaped as a fish. It was an impressive scene as a multitude of people paid their respects to a much-loved market character. As the procession left the church, all remained respectfully still. It was a very moving occasion as Dad made his final farewell journey from the place he had loved and which was so much part of his life. It was a day to remember for his family, who appreciated the kindness of so many tributes and kind messages from people who wished to celebrate his life. On the previous Friday, family members had gathered at Billingsgate Market for a traditional farewell ceremony. Silence fell among the traders and porters as they paid their respects due to the passing of a respected fishmonger. The family association with the fish trade lives on and the market stall still thrives, which is the way Dad would have wanted it.

Edward Fancourt

Four

War Stories

The Great War

My father was a victim of the First World War and I, just an infant, was left with no particular memory of him and only know of him through the stories my mother told me. Mother was left a widow with three young children and it can be imagined how she must have struggled, like so many other widows at that time, to look after us on the income provided by the state. My mother was a beautiful young widow as old photographs show, but she never remarried, only devoted herself to her children. This story was often repeated elsewhere, for, like so many others of her generation, the loss of men folk had been extreme and consequences throughout the population were immense. I had been born in 1916 and as I grew up, I looked upon my elder brother as the head of the household. Mother had of course been devastated by the loss of father in the war and always wanted to protect my brother and I from falling victim in any future hostilities. Therefore, she put my brother and I to apprenticeship with bakers, her plan that in any future war we would be protected in a 'reserved occupation', so keenly determined we would not perish as our father had. Her plan almost succeeded, for during the Second World War my brother served feeding the troops in the RAF and I was a driver, mainly serving in Northern Ireland and drove a white scout car, an American vehicle. Because of a broken wrist I was found unfit to use firearms. Both my brother and I left the army unscathed and neither of us had to go into battle throughout the war, which was a tremendous consolation for mother.

Len Hollingsworth

Lied about Age

I remember with great affection my maternal grandfather who served in the First World War. Francis Xavier Brightwell was a volunteer for the territorial army on 14 September 1914 when he was still only fifteen years of age, but his army record states 'apparent age nineteen' and it is apparent many other youngsters also gave false information to enter the armed services at that time. Eventually he served as a driver and happily came out from army service unscathed and was demobbed in 1919. Prior to his service to his country he had been employed as an electrical engineer but after he left the army he worked for Morrison's tobacco company in London, and as a driver he would deliver their products to the retailers. Later on in life he worked for the Plessey Co. in Ilford, so it was back to electronics once again. I was very fond of

'Your country needs you!' A group of soldiers who answered that call to arms, 1914–1918. (Chris Amis)

A soldier's dream of home. Mrs Faith Hollingsworth with her children, a widow of the Great War, 1914–1918. (Len Hollingsworth)

Francis Xavier Brightwell in uniform in the
First World War. (Pauline Hollingsworth)

grandad and remember he was the one who used to put my name on all my school equipment, satchels, shoes, pencil case etc. with military precision. One of the more amusing stories I remember about grandad was when, one Christmas, with all the family gathered together, he had previously and unknown to the rest of us opened some walnuts very carefully, split the shells, taken out the nut and inserted pieces of paper with jokes on, then resealed the nut. This surprise gave everyone at the table an enjoyable treat! Grandad lived a good full life until he died in his late eighties. I will always be grateful that he survived that awful war for otherwise, my own childhood memories of his kindly ways would not have been available for the retelling.

Pauline Hollingsworth (*née*) Baker

Home Front Women

My mother, Ruby Smith was one of the daughters of Walter Smith, well known at Romford Brewery. Mother married my father, Harry Sallows, a master plasterer who had served in the First World War and later in life worked on many and various buildings in Romford. A specialist plasterer, he did much work on the new cinema when the Havana Odeon Cinema was built. During the First World War, mother had worked in munitions up until the November 1918 Armistice. Auntie Rhoda, my mother's sister, did night shift duty at an engineering plant during the Second World War and I would often see her setting out to work wearing her clogs and

Faith Hollingsworth alone in Carlton Road during the Second World War. Note the taped windows. (Len Hollingsworth)

a turban on her head, popular headgear at the time. So everyone was 'doing their bit' on the home front and putting up with bombing raids during my growing up in Romford. The town had some horrendous air raids during the conflict and the brewery close by our house was hit on no fewer than five occasions. Nevertheless, it was the brewery once again that provided shelter within the buildings to protect the civilian population. I still possess my card issued to reserve a bunk place in the brewery shelter. This card bears the number ninety-one and my name and address for the public shelter at the brewery and the shelter controllers are listed as Mr Sheward and Mr Shields. The card was issued by the Borough of Romford and there were a number of listed rules to be observed, the controllers 'have the authority to eject any person behaving in an objectionable manner or otherwise causing a nuisance'; 'boots and shoes must be removed before using the bunks'; 'the shelter to be vacated not later than 7.30 a.m. (including Sundays) providing no air-raid warning is in operation in order that the shelter may be cleaned and disinfected'; these are just a few examples.

Sheila Acres (*née*) Sallows

The 'Phoney War' Period

My father was in the Army in the First World War and lost his father in one of the first air raids on London in 1916. He was convinced that the Germans would bomb Britain immediately when war broke out, therefore he arranged for the family to be evacuated to Wales to stay with relatives of our neighbours. However, we soon became homesick and returned to Romford

The Food Office staff celebrating Christmas with crepe twists, tissue bells and paper-chain decorations. (Pauline Hollingsworth)

just before Christmas in 1939. There had been no German air raids at that time, so my father judged that it was safe for us to return. This period became known as the 'Phoney War' – this changed of course as Germany invaded Denmark, Norway, Holland, Belgium and France in the spring of 1940. France capitulated in June 1940, leading to the evacuation of the British Army from Dunkirk and posing the threat of German invasion of Britain. As a boy I remember seeing an army convoy of Dunkirk returnees on the arterial road (A127) – the 'Phoney War' had ended and the Battle of Britain was about to begin.

John Strudwick

Romford's Air Training Corps Wing

In 1938, the Air League of the British Empire formed the Air Defence Cadet Corps, to inspire British youth regarding the importance of air defence matters, thus providing well-prepared recruits for the RAF and Fleet Air Arm as required. A privately funded organisation without official government support formed fifty squadrons throughout the country. Romford was the sixth unit to be formed and provided training in aviation-related subjects, as well as some military instruction studied on a part-time basis at evenings and weekends. At the outbreak of war in September 1939, many members joined the RAF and the Royal Navy's Fleet Air Arm. The services were so impressed with the quality of entrants they petitioned the government to officially sponsor the ADCC and to train older aircrew candidates awaiting call up. On 5 February 1941, the Air Ministry announced the formation of a vastly expanded organisation

When boys in uniform were turned into fighting men. (Charles Fancourt, junior)

called the Air Training Corps to succeed the ADCC. Romford's squadron became 6F, the suffix 'F' for a founding squadron. Many of the officers/instructors were First World War veterans of the RFC and RNAS, other schoolteachers and volunteer civilian instructors exempted from compulsory military service. 6F was joined by other newly formed squadrons and formed the three making up the Romford ATC Wing. Classes were held on the top floor at the Quadrant Arcade; theory of flight, Morse code, navigation and other basic RAF initial training were taught. Sunday morning parades and foot drill were done in the Plaza Cinema parking lot, often followed by a route march through the town, led by the Romford ATC Wing band.

I left school at the age of fourteen in August 1943 and worked as a junior clerk with a printing firm in London; in September that year I joined the Romford ATC by adding a year to my age to gain admittance, the minimum age was fifteen. Remaining assigned to 1943 squadron until it was disbanded in 1945 and I was transferred to 6F, still in existence today. My first opportunity to fly was December 1943 but on arrival at RAF Hornchurch we were informed of an attack on the airfield by low-flying Focke-Wulf 190 fighters, thus our flight was cancelled. However, I finally got to fly from Hornchurch in a trusty De-Havilland Dominie on an ATC air-experience flight on 17 December and we visited Hornchurch frequently for weekend camps. On one occasion we competed with a RAF regiment team in an aircraft recognition contest and beat them hands down. Also, we were given the opportunity to use a dome trainer for very realistic simulated anti-aircraft gunnery training against a Stuka dive bomber projected on a screen, giving the impression it was diving right at you, with accompanying sound track – very realistic and terrifying. ATC annual summer one-week camps on operational RAF bases were to give an idea of what serving was really like. I attended camps in 1944 and 1945 at RAF Waterbeach, near Cambridge, This was a Bomber Command Station, housing several Lancaster bomber squadrons engaged in bombing German targets every night. We were given instruction on the locations where the various activities of a working air-force base took place, the hangers where damaged aircraft were being repaired, the armoury and other sections. We lent a hand with mundane tasks, loading machine-gun belts, sweeping hanger floors and helping in the cookhouse. At dusk, we watched the Lancasters take off for their attacks on the Third Reich and many failed to return. Some were heavily damaged with wounded crew aboard. We cadets were given flights in a Lancaster bomber and I was lucky enough to find myself in a mid-upper gun turret of the plane on a day visit to RAF Tuddenham in Suffolk in early 1945. We also attended at ATC Gliding School at RAF Fairlop a few miles west of Romford. Many cadets received gliding certificates after completing the basic course satisfactorily.

John Strudwick

Chamberlain's Speech

I was a pupil at Royal Liberty School from 1938 to 1943 and lived in Romford throughout the Second World War period. My first recollection was from that unforgettable date, 3 September 1939 just after 11 a.m., having listened to Chamberlain's speech and understanding we were at war. I was helping my father erect wooden boxes filled with earth to protect the dining-room windows when the siren sounded. It is well documented that this was a false alarm, but of course we did not know that at the time and as a twelve-year-old it was quite frightening. Oddly enough, by the time of the first damage to the house in which we lived in Glenwood Drive occurred, that fear had somewhat diminished. The damage was caused by a land mine that dropped between the houses in Carlton Road, Stanley Avenue and Glenwood Drive. At the time my parents and I were sleeping on a mattress on the floor in the dining room. The sliding of tiles from the roof and then the windows being blown in woke me. I later discovered a large piece of timber from the window frame a few inches to the left-hand side of my pillow. I inspected the large crater later that morning; it had neatly fallen between five air-raid shelters that were dotted around the hole, though thankfully not one person suffered injury. There were many other raids during the ensuing years and I remember helping extinguish incendiaries but fortunately I was not personally involved in any more physical damage to property. There were many less fortunate including some friends who were killed. One of my more disconcerting activities involved the V1, or flying bomb. I recall cycling along London Road in the direction of Chadwell Heath and hearing what I thought was a petrol tanker coming up behind me. I was startled to discover a V1 about 100ft above my head. In such circumstances one hoped that the motor would last a bit longer and I was relieved that it did just that for another mile or so. Although the later V2s were more destructive and I had a few near misses, they did not cause so much fear as they arrived before the sound!

Roy Cross

Declaration of War

Although I was just over ten years old when war was declared against Germany, I was fully aware of the gravity of the situation as the country was making preparations for the expected outbreak of hostilities. As far as the civilian population in Romford was concerned these preparations took the form of installation of Anderson air-raid shelters in back gardens, the issue of gas masks to all family members and all schools had erected above ground brick shelters. I remember my mother and siblings listening to Neville Chamberlain's radio broadcast announcing Britain's declaration of war on Germany at 11 a.m. on 3 September 1939. A few minutes later the air-raid warning sounded and we ran to take cover in our air-raid shelter, donning our gasmasks, not knowing what to expect. The all clear sounded a short time after and we returned to the house for lunch. Apparently the air-raid warning was a false alarm, as a French civil aircraft on its way to Croydon failed to identify itself. At the time we were terrified, but as the war progressed in the 1940s we had become accustomed to the wailing of sirens and were no longer alarmed at the sound.

John Strudwick

Needing a Teddy Bear

I was born in Larrey House, now the Coach House Hotel, on the Main Road at the top of the Market Place in March 1940. My first clear memory is the women of the house leaning out of the top-floor windows at the back viewing south and pointing at smoke rising on the horizon. Mother picked me up so that I could see the smoke and I have assumed this was an attack on RAF Hornchurch. I next remember my mother one night rushing to get my dressing gown on with the air-raid siren wailing in the background. I particularly wanted my teddy bear before being carried downstairs to the shelter in the back garden. On another night in the air-raid shelter, my father suddenly rushed into the shelter. He was wearing a steel helmet with a white strip on it and he tried to slam and bar the door but instantly it flew open, accompanied by an explosion and something cut my cheek. Next morning everyone gathered round a hole in the nearby lawn; I believe this was an anti-aircraft shell that instead of exploding three miles up had waited until it had found itself in the lawn before the fuse worked. I remember the sound of the flying bombs which sounded like a fast-running sewing machine and the sheer terror on all the faces when the sound stopped because then the bomb was gliding downward. When one landed in Oaklands Avenue not far away, the explosion shook the dust from the shelter roof and for a few seconds faces were blurred in a mist. I also remember being evacuated – mothers and children gathered in the playground of St Edward's Senior School one morning and somehow I assumed we were bussed to Barking Station. Some forty years later I had cause to return to the station and was greeted by a nasty case of *deja vu* because suddenly I was a small boy with a Mickey Mouse gas mask, my teddy bear, a label around my neck and mum lifting me onto the train, being scared witless by the steam locomotive that seemed to leak steam from every possible place. We ended up at Croft in Leicestershire!

Patrick Arnold

Spirit of the Blitz

On the night of 10 September 1940, at the height of the Battle of Britain, the Luftwaffe jettisoned a load of bombs on Romford. One exploded at the end of our garden in Hill Grove, completely wreaking our house. In the morning, we returned from the reception centre where we had been taken after we had been recovered from our Anderson shelter. There was a gaping hole in one wall, exposing the bath in the bathroom, the skeletal roof had lost all of its tiles, curtains flapped out of empty window frames and the front door was in the back garden of the house opposite. Not only that, in true spirit of the Blitz, looters had made off with a lot of our stuff which was not actually screwed down. My mother looked at the ruins of our home at first without comment. My father was a policeman and my poor long-suffering mother had lived in four different police houses in the eight years of her marriage. Suddenly, after making a few colourful remarks about looters she said, 'I suppose this means we will be moving house yet again. It's such a pity, because I really liked this one. I wonder what the next one will be like.'

David Clark

Essex Road Bombing

It was 19 April 1941. As a small child, five years old, I was crouching, with my family, in the Anderson shelter in our garden in Essex Road. An air raid was in full swing when I remember hearing chains dragging across the roof of a garage. Moments later an almighty bang signified that a bomb had dropped very close by. In fact, two land mines with their cords tangled together had landed one each side of the road. It proved to be the biggest civilian casualty loss in one night of the war: fifty-two people died, most from Essex Road and mostly women and children. As I swung on the garden gate the following morning, I watched the soldiers of the Home Guard and the ambulance men digging furiously to find the people in the piles of rubble, occasionally hearing the name of a playmate who had been rescued or more sadly maybe died. In 2001, sixty years on, a memorial was arranged and donations enabled a figurine to be bought and placed over the altar of the local church of St John's in Mawney Road. Also a roll of honour of the names of the people who gave their lives that terrible night was placed at the side of the altar.

Hilda Bennett (*née*) Wilson

The Battle of Britain

Romford was in the direct path of German bombers following the Thames to the heart of London, the docks and many potential industrial targets. For this reason, RAF Hornchurch, North Weald and other Essex airfields housed the fighter squadrons guarding the eastern approaches to London. Because Hornchurch was seen as a prime target, the vital communications centre and operations room was transferred to the YMCA building on Western Road in Romford. As a boy I was fascinated by the sight of the many 'dog fights' taking place in the brilliant blue skies above in the form of many small silver dots and the weaving contrails and the faint sounds of gunfire. I remember seeing a downed Messerschmitt 109 fighter aircraft on display in the Plaza Cinema car park to raise money for the Spitfire Fund. It was not until Saturday afternoon on 7 September 1940 that the Luftwaffe launched a massive attack on the London Docks. I recall sighting a large number of German bombers in perfect formation proceeding east to London. I remember a neighbour saying, 'don't worry they're all ours.' That night wave after wave of bombers returned to rain down bombs on the still burning docks and the nearby Beckton gas works complex. From Romford we could see the red glow in the sky to the east of us. This was the beginning of the Night Blitz which continued until the large-scale Luftwaffe raid on London on the night of 10 May 1941, then Germany withdrew most of its bomber squadrons to Eastern Europe preparatory to its onslaught on the Eastern Front.

John Strudwick

War Years

I was born in 1931 and raised in Romford and no doubt most of my recollections of my early years will be as most people of my age dominated by experiences associated with the Second World War. The memory of sleeping night after night in the air-raid shelter at the bottom of the garden in all weathers, the noise of a mobile anti-aircraft gun running up and down the road – the disturbance was horrendous and it was very hard to try to get some sleep. One day at school I remember a German bombing raid on RAF Hornchurch with Spitfires attacking the enemy and a mighty battle ensued. The playground at the school and all around was covered with spent cannon casings and I also remember getting a clip around the ear from the teacher for staring and looking out of the window to get a better view of the cause of all this excitement. After school each day the best thing young lads knew at the time was to hunt for shrapnel and on one day we watched from a safe distance as a bomb disposal unit detonated a phosphorus bomb in the field at the rear of our houses. Later I retrieved some shrapnel from this area and took my trophy to school and while it lay in the heat of my desk I discovered it had ignited and was covered with a vivid blue flame, so I had to take it and bury it in the school flower beds and I sometimes wonder if it could still be there!

Derek 'Del' Osborne

Cold Comfort

Going to work in Romford was anything but quiet during the war, daylight raids interrupted work as we took off for the air-raid shelter, plus the night raids when my mother and I had been up half the night. Seeing as I had to be at work by 7.30 a.m. each morning it was an effort, as bleary eyed and sometimes unwashed, having slept in our clothes, the next day dawned. Never mind, we got on with it. In the winter it was perishing, heating was from a coal fire in the dining room and hot water available from a kettle boiled on the gas stove. The alarm clock sounded like the hammer of doom in the dark and frosty mornings and I grabbed my clothes to change, into the bed just to warm them up. The bedroom was nigh on freezing and one's breath condensed into little clouds of vapour. I cooked my own breakfast, usually porridge with a dribble of treacle and a slice of bread and margarine with homemade preserve. So then it was on my bike to work. In those early war years we were on double summertime and single summertime in winter. One dark, frosty and slippery morning I was cycling to work when an early-morning air raid was on, my bike displayed shrouded paraffin lamp front and rear as it was impossible to buy batteries. The bike skidded, I fell on my back, the paraffin lamp's spilt oil on the road and ignited. Shouts of 'put that light out' was bawled at me as I danced a fandango in the road trying to stamp out the flames, fortunately no traffic about as of course petrol was rationed at that time. Then one morning at the end of 1942 my call-up papers arrived, there were four postal deliveries a day in those times. So I was off to join the RNAS or Fleet Air Arm at Squires Gate, near Blackpool.

Chris Amis

Two Came Home

During the Second World War my Uncles Wally and Bert Smith were called up to serve His Majesty King George VI in the armed forces. Uncle Wally was away from the Romford Brewery

Bert Smith in uniform. He was captured in the desert and imprisoned in German Stalag. (Sheila Acres)

Wally Smith found himself landing on the Normandy beaches for the invasion of Europe, 1944. (Sheila Acres)

serving with the Pioneers, he took part in the Normandy landings on D-Day plus one, 7 June 1944. The landings in France were such a deciding factor in the outcome of the war and the allied invasion became known as the D-Day landings. Many lives were lost during the invasion but happily we were able to welcome both our boys home after the war ended. Uncle Bert, who had attended St Edward's School in Romford did his war service with the Royal Artillery and using his experience as a driver at the Ind Coope Brewery, was sent to the western desert as an army lorry driver. Unfortunately he was captured behind enemy lines and thereafter remained a POW (prisoner of war) in a German Stalag until liberated in 1945 when they were happily returned to their families and also their former working life at the brewery, resuming their role in the distribution of beer.

Sheila Acres (*née*) Sallows

A Lucky Escape

On the evening of 30 June 1944, my father had left duty and had a meal after another long day at the police station and was looking forward to an early night. He was living alone my mother and three children had been evacuated to Derbyshire for our safety away from the air raids. On the way home he called to see friends, Mr and Mrs Gent, who ran the sub-post office and shop at Roneo Corner. They had been given a freshly shot rabbit but had no idea how to prepare it for the table. Many a rabbit at this time met a premature end as a supplement to the meagre wartime rations. Dad, a country boy, was only too pleased to oblige, he gutted, skinned and jointed the rabbit ready for the pot. His good deed had delayed his intended return home for an early night and as he was about to leave, now around the time he would have been in bed, a large explosion appeared to come from the direction of our home in Victoria Road. Immediately he got on his bicycle and pedalled down Park Lane and Albert Road to Victoria Road, he realised the explosion had been a 'doodlebug'. It dropped on the railway embankment near our house, fortunately there were no casualties. Dad got home to find the entire window frame in the front bedroom had been blown in and broken glass and wreckage had landed on the bed where he would have been, had he not made sure that Mr and Mrs Gent got their rabbit pie!

David Clark

Far Away Island

During the Second World War my father had travelled extensively first to France, Belgium and Holland then on to Cape Town and finally shipped south to the Falkland Islands. A destination very well known to us from the later Falklands War conflict, but people rarely associate the fact that we had a Falkland Island force out in the South Atlantic Sea during the Second World War.

I have a Christmas greeting card, an official issue, which he sent home to my mother in 1942. When he returned home on an embarkation leave it was bittersweet, the family knowing he was about to join a fighting force and in fact he joined the Allies in the invasion of Europe. After the war my mother was so pleased to welcome him home at last and together they were happy in the years they spent together in Romford with a boy and a girl to complete the family. I treasure all his wartime memorabilia and have made a collage of his service photographs and his medals, which I proudly display in my home.

Ellen Preston (*née*) Huggett

Bert Huggett, posted to the Falkland Islands, sent a Christmas greeting home to wife from the Falkland Force, 1942. (Ellen Preston)

Ellen Preston has made this collage of her father's war. He served in European campaigns prior to duty in the Falklands then returned for the invasion of Europe. (Ellen Preston)

The Blitz

My family moved to a new house in Cedar Road, Romford, in 1930 where I lived prior to emigration to Canada and the US in 1957, my memories of the town are many and the blitz years stand out. Large-scale Luftwaffe night raids continued for over eight months although daytime attacks were reduced somewhat. Romford tried to settle to a normal routine and children were regularly attending school. I was attending Pettits Lane School when after morning assembly the air-raid warning sounded on most days requiring orderly procession to the shelters. Each shelter held 100 persons and was lit by a solitary light bulb. Teachers continued with our lessons but it was difficult to concentrate with noise of falling bombs and anti-aircraft gunfire outside. We actually had a 3.7in gun installed in the sports field behind the school. During a night raid, a German oil bomb demolished the chemical laboratory and chemistry lessons ceased for lack of replacement equipment during the war and most cheered Adolf Hitler for that. After daytime raids we returned home for quick supper then into the shelter at the bottom of the garden ready for the night attacks. In the morning we woke to the all clear siren, back to the house, wash, dress and breakfast, then back to school. This became a routine until after 10 May 1941 when Hitler's attention turned eastwards and postponed any invasion plans. One tragic night, Saturday 19 April 1941, my father was working night shift at Oldham's Press in London, mother was preparing the shelter for the night and it was raining hard. I heard German bombers overhead and noise like chains rattling, scooping up my baby sister I ran with all my might through torrential rain into the shelter. My arrival accompanied by two tremendous explosions caused by parachute mines, one landed in Essex Road the other hit Cedric Avenue with horrendous fatalities, and the people of Romford were horrified. Most German assaults after May 1941 were hit-and-run nuisance raids by single aircraft causing few casualties or property damage. However, one morning in 1943 a Focke-Wulf 190 fighter raked Romford Railway Station with cannon fire, fortunately no London-bound commuters were injured. Early in 1944 my brother, David and I set out for Stapleford Abbots to collect souvenirs from a crashed Junkers 88 bomber on a farm but we were chased off empty handed by a Home Guard sentry! Thereafter, from June 1944 Romford suffered many attacks by V1 flying bombs and V2 rockets causing many casualties and much damage.

John Strudwick

Raid on Romford

Between the blitz ending and the first V1s or doodlebugs, air raids on Romford were sporadic. But, just after breakfast 12 March 1943, we suddenly heard low-flying aircraft and gunfire from the direction of Romford Station a few hundred yards from our house in Victoria Road. Looking out of the window my father and I saw a German Focke-Wulf 190 with a Spitfire on his tail flying fast at rooftop height over two cottages in Shaftesbury Road, which backed on to our garden. I remember the occupants were Mr and Mrs Huggins and Mr and Mrs Richardson at the time. My memory is vivid of the green fuselage, its sinister black cross and it was so close, the helmeted head of the German pilot in his cockpit. Gone in a flash, but from the street we could see that one of the gasholders at Romford Gas Works was on fire, smoke coming from half-way up the side. In fact a dozen Focke-Wulf 190s had flown from northern France on a daylight raid, at the Essex coast they spilt into two flights of six, one attacked the RAF night fighter station at Bradwell Bay and the other flew up the Thames to attack the

Plessey factory at Ilford. These Focke-Wulf 190s were the fighter-bomber version, they carried 500kg (1,100lb) bomb under the fuselage and cannon and machine guns in the wings and nose. Plessey's factory was not hit – the bombs appear to have been dropped at random on the centre of Ilford, killing thirty-one people, injuring forty-three and rendering many homeless. On return the German aircraft used cannon and machine guns at random, flying over Romford they shot up the gasholders and railway station. The 7.15 a.m. Liverpool Street was about to leave, when the platform and train were strafed, but miraculously nobody was hurt. The RAF was airborne in hot pursuit, the records unclear from where they came but probably from Biggin Hill. The other flight of six Focke-Wulfs attacked RAF Bradwell Bay but the raid was unsuccessful as their bombs fell in open countryside, unfortunately one person was killed. The raid foiled by a Norwegian squadron based at North Weald, which chased them out to the sea and claimed all six had been shot down. One German plane on the way out machine gunned the Thames sailing barge *Alaric* which had just left Burnham-on-Crouch, killing the master, Henry Eves, but his son uninjured sailed the barge back to Burnham. Today, if you approach the gas works from Crow Lane, the patches riveted to the side of the gasholder are still there to see. The fires were put out and the holes repaired by a courageous fireman wearing an asbestos suit. He managed to work against the clock for four hours with the danger of the gasholder imploding when all the gas was burnt off and the inside became a vacuum. The two cottages in Shaftesbury Road were demolished in the 1960s to make way for Manor Primary School when Albert Road Primary School closed and moved round the corner to its new location.

David Clark

Laughing Sailor Boys

Two of my uncles, Uncle Stan and Uncle 'Boy', were both in the Royal Navy during the Second World War. Uncle Stan volunteered for the Royal Navy in 1943 aged seventeen and served on several ships including HMS *Le Fantasque*, eventually becoming a leading telegraphist on board prior to his demob in December 1946. His brother Francis, always known as 'Boy' within the family at Pemberton Road, Gidea Park, also joined the Royal Navy and served as a signalman on HMS *Ramillies*. Both happily returned unscathed after the war and came home to the family. My memories of them are happy ones and they always were very kind to me as a child and were indeed perfect uncles. I recall wonderful days on the beach with mother and her brothers I just remember them always jolly and laughing. One particular event I remember when I was around nine years old was when Uncle 'Boy' and his wife Auntie Beryl took me on a holiday with them and their two children to a bungalow in Jaywick. I remember I had bought myself a blow-up beach ball from Woolworth's and was very proud of my new possession. But the very first time I played with it at the bungalow garden it landed in the wire fence and to my dismay burst. Uncle 'Boy' immediately came to the rescue, taking me at once back to Woolworth's, bought a bicycle puncture-repair kit and mended it for me.

Pauline Hollingsworth (*née*) Baker

Window Flowers

My family ran the butchers shop at 31, Victoria Road, during the war at the time the V1 dropped on the railway embankment nearby which caused us to be 'bombed out' temporarily, but we

Stan and 'Boy' Brightwell, Royal Navy sailors on leave at Pemberton Gardens, Gidea Park. (Pauline Hollingsworth)

Soldier! soldier! Len Hollingsworth in Army uniform. (Pauline Hollingsworth)

Another hero – John Thorogood, who lost his life serving with the RAF, as did his brother. The War Office were requested by the parents to spare them one son who happily returned home safely. (Pauline Hollingsworth)

were fortunate as the property next door was destroyed. After the war was over my father bought the bombsite and turned it into a garden area with a rockery made with some of the rubble. There he grew flowers and after the week's trading in meat was done, he would make a floral display to exhibit in the shop window on Sundays. So eye catching were these skilful floral arrangements that many people thought that he was a professional florist and wanted to buy them! Not to be outdone, I also exhibited my Meccano efforts alongside Dad's flowers.

Peter Copsey

Victory in Europe

Just before 11 a.m. on the morning of 8 May 1945 we children were celebrating our precious fifteen minutes of playtime in the playground of Moss Lane Infants' School. A short, plump lady with black hair and an armful of bunting and flags came running past our school gate shouting: 'Unconditional surrender! The Germans have surrendered! The war is over!' Immediately, the teacher on playground duty ran into the school to spread the news. We all broke out cheering and dancing *Ring a Ring o' Roses*. A bit dubious as I did not know what 'unconditional' meant. However, suitably reassured later by Mum, I was ready to join the celebrations that evening. A huge bonfire was built in the road at the junction of Albert Road and Shaftesbury Road. All sorts of things went on the bonfire, wood, cardboard boxes, garden rubbish and even a couple of kitchen chairs. My father was the police officer in charge of security in Romford throughout the war and as such he

Victory at last! Celebrations everywhere included street parties for the children. (Charles Fancourt, junior)

Len Hollingsworth reunited at last with family. (Len Hollingsworth)

A statue from the Italian Embassy was bought at a reparation auction after the war. It stood in a garden in Romford until resold to the embassy. The staff were delighted to recover it. (Muriel Arnold)

had access to all the fireworks, which had been impounded in September 1939 and locked in the police station ever since. On their release, we were treated to a grand impromptu firework display. We had never seen fireworks before and were thrilled. Eventually the tarmac under the bonfire caught fire and we had an even bigger blaze than expected! Scores of people there were singing favourite wartime songs *Roll out the Barrel* and *We're Going to Hang out the Washing on the Seigfried Line*. The next day, like many other families in Victoria Road, we hung a large Union Flag out of a bedroom window. But the damaged road surface in Albert Road that marked the site of our bonfire stayed there as a reminder of that joyful night for many years to come.

David Clark

Japanese Experience

My father along with many others had the most horrendous experiences during the war when he became a prisoner of the Japanese upon the fall of Singapore, 15 February 1942. From early 1942 to the summer of 1944 he was working on the infamous 'Railway of Death' until its completion and could not believe his good fortune at returning to Singapore after nearly two years of hell in disease-stricken jungle camps from where so many would never return. Firstly work was done at the docks when a German submarine arrived and the crew, so appalled at their physical condition, gave them food daily while docked there. Marched to a vessel to embark for Japan the cramped

'Lest we forget'. The war memorial at the top of the Market Place with poppy tributes, November 2007. (Patricia Pound)

conditions on board were appalling, many prisoners suffering with dysentery and malaria would obviously not survive the journey. Four days out at sea, the convoy was attacked, by submarines, the attack came at dusk, depth charges echoed like thunder each time as though the ship had been hit, the prisoners were trapped like rats below decks. After three days of attacks, my Dad on a trip to the latrine on deck, saw obvious signs of damage and preparations to abandon ship, the decision to go over the side, while the armed crew was in panic running about the decks, was soon taken. Meeting up with other English prisoners on a raft in the oil-thick waters, together they watched the ship go down. After many hours in the life raft eventually Dad was picked up by a Japanese frigate – many others not so fortunate were left in the sea, their chances pretty hopeless. Arriving in Hainan port, they were transported again on a whaling factory ship to Formosa. Unable to leave there until the third attempt and then having to call in at Moji where they rested in stables and were given a meal. Train to Tokyo then to northern Japan, where he worked as a slave labourer, in a cold winter climate on various unpleasant projects. Hard work and starvation rations were the order of his days, the air-raid attacks got more frequent, the camp was hit by incendiary bombs. Pandemonium broke out at that time and the news that the war had ended was later given to them by the camp commander. They impatiently awaited the Allies who at last sent planes, which parachuted huge canisters filled with food, tobacco, medical supplies and everything needed. The war had ended – Dad was liberated by the Americans in 1945, recuperated in New Zealand for several weeks, arriving at Southampton Docks 6 January 1946. He was reunited with his wife who he had not seen for five years, my mother, Ann Mole, his wife, refused to accept the government war widow's pension in 1944, refusing to believe him dead. He worked in Romford for many years involved with the café in the Romford Shopping Hall, The Tea Pot which is still in family hands. Only reluctantly did he tell his story to a family member before he died 26 July 1995 aged eighty-one.

Jackie Wallace (*née*) Mole

Five

A Sporting Life

Archer Leggett

Archer Leggett, the man who founded the famous Romford Greyhound Stadium, kept his dogs in the stables at the rear of the house called Elmhurst at Collier Row and the very first greyhound track was set up in the field behind the house. Mr Reader from Ireland was his trainer and a real character. Sacking was nailed to hedge stakes to form a screen. The first race on 21 June 1929 attracted only fifty or sixty spectators but they decided the meetings were successful and decided to move their operations to London Road and the stadium stands were in place in 1931. The stadium has seen many a fine race since and has played a part in the history of the town, including when Mr Leggett bought cheetahs from Kenya in December 1937 and started racing them, the first time this had happened in England.

Muriel Arnold (*née*) Lilley

More Than a Living

As well as a fair living, the brewery provided many sporting facilities and events for the work force. Not only was there an immaculate bowling green, which my grandad maintained with pride for a number of years, but facilities for quoits competitions and many other sports including the lovely sports field for football and cricket matches. These matches would therefore embrace other sports teams around the town and so many people will still remember happy days at the sports ground. Sadly, this is now just a memory for all is gone, together with the company itself, which was once so much part of our lives in Romford. During the 1960s this area of the brewery was demolished during a building expansion to increase production. It was a sad day when the bulldozers tore up that beautiful bowling green, which grandad had loved. The brewery however provided an alternative sports ground at Whalebone Lane, although that too is now gone.

Sheila Acres (*née*) Sallows

Brewery Cricket Ground

My father used to play in the Romford Police Cricket XI, whose home ground was at the brewery. When there was a mid-week match on, I would make my way there after school and

The Romford Police Cricket Team, 1948. Back row, left to right: standing in suit, Detective Sergeant F.D. Clark, fifth from left, PC Dick Neale (coroner's officer), sixth from left, PC Fred Northover, seventh from left, Inspector Hancock. Seated: fourth from left, Inspector Les Green, fifth from left PC Hunter. (David Clark)

A Glendale F.C. youth team. Back row, standing first on the left, Ron Fuller. (Ron Fuller)

help the scorer in his hut. I used to pass the numbers to him so that he could hang them on the scoreboard. My particular favourite was the picture of the duck. I was aged about ten at the time.

David Clark

Glendale F.C. Youth Teams

Glendale had three teams, two for under eighteen year olds and one for under sixteens and was Romford Town's Football Club's youth team in the 1950s. During the late 1940s and 1950s Romford Football Club was regarded as one of the best amateur clubs in the country and had a huge following at their Brooklands Stadium. They reached the first amateur cup final to be played at Wembley, unfortunately losing 1–0 to Bromley. Glendale played in Hornchurch and district youth league and won on numerous occasions and often had scouts watching from professional clubs. The youth team were allowed to train one evening a week at the Romford ground under floodlights, which at that time were only at one end of the ground. Even so, this was quite a new innovation and the lads certainly felt privileged. In 1955/56 season, Glendale played in the F.A. Youth Cup where they met West Ham United youth team at the Brooklands ground. Although the local team lost, they were up against a number of players who a few years later went on to win the F.A. Cup and European Cup Winners' Cup for the great West Ham United side of 1964/65.

Ron Fuller

Football at Brooklands

My family were all great supporters of our local football teams with good memories of visits to Brooklands football ground off Mawney Road, between Brooklands Road and Drummond Road. In 1948 the whole town was immensely excited, as our Romford team was to go to Wembley to compete in the F.A. Amateur Cup Final against Bromley. Many families including my own were determined to attend at Wembley Stadium to cheer our local team and give our encouragement and loyal support to our boys. What a disappointment when we lost to Bromley 1–0 although loyal Romfordians were convinced that our boys had played the better game.

Sheila Acres (*née*) Sallows

Football with Father

When Romford was playing at home, my father would take me to see them play at Brooklands. Romford was an amateur team, with captain Jim Paviour, the goalkeeper Reg Ivey, a metropolitan policeman. Before the match, we would hear their signature tune played over the public address system. It was Donald Peers singing *By a Babbling Brook* which of course referred to the River Rom which flowed near the ground. The crowd was always good-humoured, but you did hear the occasional shout of 'tread on his neck!' or 'put him in a glass case!'

Romford's hour of glory came in 1949 when they played Bromley in the final at Wembley Stadium, in the presence of the Earl and Countess of Athlone. We lost 1–0 but it was a good

The Royal Liberty School play the beautiful game. Team member Charles Fancourt, junior, is on the second row seated fourth from left. (Charles Fancourt, junior)

hard-fought game. I remember on the way home on the tube, my father discussing with his friend, whether HMS *Amethyst* would ever fight its way out of the Yangtze River.

David Clark

Sport of Kings

When dreams of a football career had been put to one side I became interested in horse racing which expanded into a passion for the sport, which was to include ownership with friends. Later joining syndicates at Newmarket when breeding, selling and racing horses was continued with a fair bit of success. My proudest moment came when one of our horses, Wavertree Boy, raced in the oldest classic race in the world, the St Ledger (named for Lord Wavertree who had given the national stud to the country). Our current partnership in the national stud is known as the 'Never Say Die' syndicate, named for that famous Derby winner which was ridden by the eighteen-year-old, Lester Piggott in 1954, making him the youngest jockey to win the race. This interest has never given the richest money rewards but the pleasure the horse has provided in my life is beyond price, embracing all aspects of following training to attending races. Not forgetting other less fortunate horses ending their days in retirement at charity run sanctuaries,

I have happily volunteered for mucking-out duties and spent some time just enjoying being around horses.

Ron Fuller

A Sportsman

Apart from running a successful market business as a fishmonger, my Dad will long be remembered in Romford for his contribution and enthusiasm for the Romford Bowls Club. My father, Charlie Fancourt, was president of the club for many years, from the days at the old Kings Head ground in the Market Place through to the move to the present ground at Lodge Farm Park. He enjoyed great success as a bowler and won a number of club and county competitions and also became president of Essex County Bowls Association and for several years he was an active member of the Havering Sports Council. Both my brother Edward and I together with our sister Annette grew up with a strong sporting background and it is something that I was immensely interested in when I as a younger man, gaining team place in various sports teams when at the Royal Liberty School. I was pleased to try and emulate Dad and with his encouragement enjoyed a fair amount of success myself. Later joining the Romford Golf Club I was among the winning team of the Essex County Amateur Golf Championship Thornton Cup 1969 and the Thornton Cup Finalists in 1976. My wife, Joyce, was also a member and won the Petre Cup in 1972, we both loved the game and the camaraderie and the social functions were also enjoyed, but the sport was the principal factor. In 1981 my wife was Lady Captain and in the same year I won the captain's prize. My brother Edward shared the love of the game and in 1986 won four trophies in one year, quite a feat! Edward was captain in 1997 and my son Charles also a member, made it a quartet of family members. I think our success was very pleasing for Dad.

Charles Fancourt, junior

Marks & Spencer

My mother worked at one time for the department store in the 1930s and they provided many facilities for their staff over time from staff hairdressing to canteen facilities. During her time of service they were many sports activities arranged and she took part in their netball and handball teams with great enthusiasm. I feel this was a forerunner of the present-day practice of encouraging staff to partake in joint activities to create good attitudes to improve relationships and create team spirit in the workplace.

Lesley Godbold (née) Gage

Romford Bowls Club members and it is Romford v The Rest. (Fancourt Family)

Romford Bowls Club – bowling woods! (Fancourt Family)

Romford Bowls Club – new beginnings at Lodge Farm Park. (Fancourt Family)

Members of Romford Golf Club, which was established in 1894 and still flourishing as a highly respected golf club. (Fancourt Family)

President of Romford Bowls Association presents the Charles Fancourt Trophy. (Fancourt Family)

Marks & Spencer ladies' netball team, 1930s. (Lesley Godbold)

Marks & Spencer – a game of handball with a super-size ball, 1930s. (Lesley Godbold)

Driving an Army truck on National Service combined with sporting opportunities for Ron Fuller.
(Ron Fuller)

Taught to Ski

In the 1950s I was 'called up' to serve two years in the Army and, leaving Seymer Road, I reported as ordered, passed a medical and got my wish to serve with the Royal Artillery. Initial training in north Wales was pretty tough but on being posted to Germany I was pleased to be able to play football for the regiment. Posted on to Winterberg, a ski centre for the British forces, I was delighted with the opportunity to learn to ski well. The following year I represented the regiment in the Army ski championships but failed to distinguish myself on that occasion, finishing well down the field. A few of the best skiers were considered for the Olympic ski team. My skiing was not going to take me to those dizzy heights but it endowed me with a lifelong passion for the sport, which I have been able to enjoy throughout the years. I had been fortunate with my service as destinations were a bit of a lottery and I could have ended up in a much more troublesome spot.

Ron Fuller

Six

That's Entertainment

Church Hall Comedy

The Laurie Cinema, later The Vogue at the top of the Market Place, was still operating into the 1950s. Although the cinema memory that stands out in my mind and a much earlier experience, was when, along with friends I would go to Roneo corner area, where early on a Friday evening in a church hall 'one reeler' Charlie Chaplin, Buster Keaton, or similar films were shown. Providing you had a penny for entrance or an empty jam jar and were willing to join in a couple of hymns before the show began, you could enjoy the comedy films – it was a favourite outing when I was a child. Empty jam jars were accepted as admission fee, as a penny was redeemable when returned to the shops. We would walk the distance from Rush Green on unmade roadway at that time, without adults and this was perfectly acceptable and normal and I can never remember being fearful on my travels.

Judy Smith (*née*) Watters

The Circus

Romford used to have an annual visit from a traditional old-time tented circus, an event eagerly awaited by young and old. I was about four years old in the early 1930s when father took me to Lord George Sanger's Circus. The tent was pitched on a vacant lot near Oldchurch Hospital. I was truly impressed with the performance and the elephants, lions and tigers displayed in their cages. When war broke out in 1939 all travelling circuses ceased for the duration. These days the circus coming to town is a rare event; some objections to caged animals performing in this way have limited this way of life.

John Strudwick

Drama Days

Now in my nineties, I fondly day dream as I turn the pages of my scrapbooks, remembering the days when I was fortunate enough to have leading roles in many a performance with the Red Triangle Drama Group. Especially the productions we were involved with during the years of the Second World War, at that time we could fill the theatre with an audience three nights

Treading the boards was a long-term love for 'Stevie' Edmonds who had many a starring role with the Red Triangle Dramatic Association. (Patricia Pound)

of the week. Our audiences keen for diversion from the realities of a wartime existence and the play was the thing! Another main entertainment being the wireless broadcasts listened to at home. The distraction and the companionship we thespians found in the amateur dramatic comradeship we found together, was no less a lifeline for us, in keeping us busy rehearsing and performing for our appreciative audiences. The range of plays we performed were classics, very well-known playwrights and local productions of famous 'hits' of the day were very popular indeed. After the war ended, diverse forms of entertainment were once again available and of course the coming of television, an essential in many homes in the 1950s. The company finally dwindled for multiple reasons not least the passing years but nevertheless my eyes linger over the photographs of once familiar friends and times gone by and I remember happy days.

'Stevie' Edmonds

Millie Martin

When my older sister Margaret was a pupil at Heath Park School Secondary School in the late 1940s, she was always coming home from school with tales about a particularly high-spirited classmate who appeared to be the bane of the teachers' lives. This girl was often in trouble and appeared to have little respect for authority. The girl was named Millie Martin and as a small boy I was dazzled by the ease with which my sister and her friends from school turned effortless cartwheels in our garden. One of them was Millie! Even at school, Millie was outstanding in theatre productions and her burning ambition was to go on the stage. It was with some measure of relief, I believe, that the staff at Heath Park learned that Millie had won a place at the Italia Conti Academy. She obviously did well there as the next I heard of her was about 1955 when the

It all starts at school – children at London Road School present *Mother Goose*, 1950s. (Lesley Godbold)

name, Millicent Martin, was on a hoarding at Gallows Corner, advertising the West End show *Hit the Deck*. This was about the time that she had what was known at the time as a 'Myrna Loy' nose job. Since then her face has been known to millions through her work on television and in the theatre. In 1961 she burst onto our TV screens in *That Was The Week That Was,* the show that heralded in the age of satire and the social revolution of the Swinging Sixties.

David Clark

Carrying a Torch

I now live with my husband and family in Australia, we flew out as '£10 poms' and celebrated our golden wedding anniversary in 2003 at a German restaurant The Cuckoo in the Dandenong Ranges where we live. We married in Romford and although that was obviously a good while ago I still have great memories of my young days in the town. At one time I worked as an usherette at the Gaumont Cinema in South Street; it was almost opposite what was then Sainsbury's store. I worked with a great bunch of people and we girls had a lot of fun shining our torches on the couples in the back row, usually catching them in the beam of torchlight having a kiss and a cuddle, which is what couples did in the darkened cinema back then. In 1952 the cinema entered a float in the Romford carnival parade and my friends and I were dressed as Hawaiian hula girls and one of our girls won the beauty crown that year. After the carnival we had a visit from a popular actor at that time, Harry Fowler – he was in many British films and we were thrilled to meet 'a star'. We had fun listening to and laughing at his jokes as he was a very funny guy! He appeared recently in a television 'soap' over here, he had aged somewhat but then I remembered, so have we all! I now know the cinema is long gone but the memories live on.

Sheila Osborne (née) Pendley

End of the pier show at Bridlington. Second from left is Joan Howard aged fourteen on stage with Dad, 'Mad Horse' Howard, far right. (Joan Howard)

Sweet Charity

My father, Laurie Howard, performed on stage all over the world from end of pier shows to music hall, from the Alhambra, Leicester Square, to Proctors on Broadway, New York City, a music-hall variety act sometimes billed as a comedian but also as 'Mad Horse' for his famous clog dance act when he imitated a horse! I was born into this show-business world – my godfather was the great actor manager Sir Edward Seymour Hicks and I joined my father on stage at the age of eight, lived in showbiz 'digs' and lost count of all the schools I attended. Sadly both my parents died young, father aged fifty and mother aged forty. I met and married my husband Reg within three months of our first meeting and when we came to Harold Hill, with the roar of the crowd and grease paint flowing in my veins, we founded the famous 'Hilltones' variety group in 1966. This great group of volunteers have raised thousands of pounds for charity over the years. After more than forty years now, the 'high kicks' are not what they were, but with Peter Brown as singer and compère still fronting the show, there are still bookings coming in for 2008! My thanks to the lovely 'family' of dedicated people who gave their time and energy to making the 'Hilltones' such a great success story.

Joan Howard

The Hilltones

In the 1960s not long after Joan Howard and husband Reg had realised a dream to create an all singing, all-dancing group to raise funds for charity, I joined their number. A glittering extravaganza, the hallmark of the 'Hilltones' variety group provided a line up of glamour girls ably assisted by a few men, producing entertainment for audiences in many locations throughout Essex. We successfully raised thousands of pounds for various charities over the years, still continuing to the present day. At the height of their success the couple celebrated their diamond wedding in 2001,

Above: The joy of giving. The Hilltones present a cheque to the local St Francis Hospice. (Joy Blackmur)

Right: For Joan Howard and husband Reg, founders of the Hilltones, there was 'no business like show business'. (Joan Howard)

Glamour girls galore! Peter Brown presents the Hilltones. (Joy Blackmur)

at that time Reg was a youthful eighty-two and Joan was seventy-nine and insisted there were plenty more dancing years ahead! Based at Harold Hill, we rehearsed regularly and went from strength to strength, David 'Diddy' Hamilton named us a top team on his show, we performed everything from old-time music-hall shows, to famous musicals to Christmas pantomime, in nursing homes, hospitals and at the Queens Theatre, Hornchurch. Sadly Reg died, but in true tradition the show went on. Show business was in her blood and Joan had been a professional from childhood, she was so proud of her father who was on the bill at the Stratford Empire with the great Marie Lloyd in the 1920s. With her great stage presence, drive and enthusiasm, Joan has done tremendous work and inspired the troupe throughout the years and a great round of applause and a big 'thank you' is due to Joan Howard. I have been proud to have been part of this great line up and will continue to tread the boards with the 'Hilltones' as long as I am able.

Joy Blackmur (*née*) Williams

Strictly Ballroom

In my teens like many others I felt it very necessary to learn how to dance 'properly' and I attended the Albert Rudge Dance School. The venue for the lessons was above the Odeon Cinema on the corner of Havana Close and I enjoyed learning all the traditional dance steps, which was to prove such an asset in my adult social life. The 'twist' and disco dancing came later. Out of favour for so long the TV programme *Strictly Come Dancing* has revived the interest in ballroom which everyone was keen to learn at my ballroom dancing classes. Of course there were also many Saturday night hops then, dances at the Wykeham Hall and the Willow Rooms in Mawney Road and many more besides. Often these venues had live music bands and a master of ceremonies and many lifetime partners met under the revolving glitter ball of the dance hall.

Ellen Preston (née) Huggett

All That Jazz

In 1955, aged seventeen I was a member of the 2nd Romford Scout Troop, together with five other scouts we became interested in jazz. We then with very little knowledge, decided to form a band. The open-minded Scout committee gave permission for practice in the scout hall. Most of us acquired our first instruments from the Pioneer Sales and Service shop in Seven Kings, an Aladdin's cave to us and were later delighted when a branch opened in North Street, Romford, opposite the Betterwear Brush Factory. Ian Kirkaldy bought a battered trumpet, Ian Holmes was given a trombone by his uncle, Alan Clare for some reason decided to construct his own double bass, which had one string and was one step from a 'tea-chest' bass. I promised myself a guitar when I passed my driving test and when I did it was straight to Pioneer Sales and Service for my instrument. During our awful first practices as we came to terms with how to hold, blow or strum these strange bits of brass and wood. We started our practice behind the stage curtains at the scout hall, but after some complaints, moved to a room over Taylor's Restaurant near Market Place. Eventually our first public performances were at the British Legion Hall in Collier Row. Our next residency, a cellar in Ilford High Street, down steep steps through cellar doors and here

Scout Camp at Gerrards Cross, 1957. Aspiring musicians playing non-existent instruments they thought they wanted to play, all ending up playing something different. (Pete Bernard)

Serious pose on Scout Hall stage – the whole band present for the photo call, 1957. (Pete Bernard)

we played to capacity crowds in this smoky, dark damp hole and loved every minute of it. A year later we were offered gigs in the holy grail of British New Orleans jazz, the Ken Colyer Club, just off Charing Cross Road. All-night sessions in another dark claustrophobic cellar but, 'hey' we could handle this, we had arrived! It was a challenge not only musically but also logistically – we had no transport other than public buses and trains. What dedication when we carried basses, drum kits etc. down to Romford Station, thence via train and tube to places as far away as Clapham. On occasion this caused chaos when drums would bounce down escalators but we were young, it was all just fun, a step up from the bikes we had used at local gigs. We had also used the two-wheeled scout trek cart when available to transport drums etc. to the station and it was just as well we could not afford amplification gear. In 1958 we had the pleasure of returning to the Scouts to play at our Scoutmaster's farewell party when he was emigrating to Australia. Was the music so bad he had to go that far! I sincerely thank the Scouts for the encouragement of our musical aspirations, for music has continued to play a very important part in my life and career to date. Not forgetting all the other lessons learned and the wonderful camping trips too! I hope scouting still thrives at Ashby Hall in Mawney Road and often wonder if any other bands started there – and what would Baden-Powell have thought of Scouts embracing the jazz life?

Pete Barnard

Children's Theatre

During the 1960s, I joined the Romford Children's Theatre, an amateur theatre company. They produced and performed plays in schools and children's homes. Transporting scenery

The very successful Romford Children's Theatre present *Tobias and the Angel*, 1960s. (Pauline Hollingsworth)

Shakespeare in the Park performed at Raphael's Park natural amphitheatre, 1960s. The audience is seated in Romford Borough Council deckchairs. (Pauline Hollingsworth)

Marks & Spencer dancing troupe stepping out to entertain, 1930s. (Lesley Godbold)

Sharon Osborne gave her time generously to encourage little ones at dance school. (Alison Burkett)

with a furniture van, we set up, gave performance, the set was struck and put back in the van all in one night, driven off to the next venue for repeat performance next day. Many performers and stage crew were in full-time work outside of these duties! I remember a performance of *The Tinder Box* – an actor dressed as a dog bounded onto stage, jumped onto a bed, which immediately collapsed. Audience thought it brilliant, part of the show, we had many letters saying how clever! Joining other theatre companies we performed *Shakespeare in the Park* in the natural amphitheatre in Raphael's Park, where I took part in *As You Like It*. My thanks to all who made it possible.

Pauline Hollingsworth (*née*) Baker

Shall we Dance?

I trained at the Bush Davis Dance Academy in Eastern Road, and had a successful career and now running dance schools, teaching all forms of dance. Recently, Sharon Osborne delighted our children when she was guest of honour for prize-giving presentations. The pupils were thrilled to meet this famous lady and Sharon was delightful giving time generously, showing interest, and giving her encouragement to all. She made it a lovely occasion for everyone present.

Alison Burkett (*née*) Haynes

Seven

All our Yesterdays

The Great Depression

I was born in 1929 just in time for the Great Depression, it started in New York with the crash in October of that year and spread worldwide and did not really end until just before the outbreak of the Second World War. I remember very well in the mid-1930s, seeing long lines of unemployed men outside the employment exchange in North Street waiting to collect the 'dole.' My father in a secure job decided in 1930 to purchase a three-bedroom house in Cedar Road in the Brooklands area of Romford for £600! The housing estate was built on farmland and Cedar Road was not yet paved. Mother told me she often had to chase cows and sheep out of the garden, which came through a gap in the hawthorn hedge on our boundary. At a later date the land behind our property became the home of the Romford Football Club.

John Strudwick

The Golden Mile

South Street was known as the Golden Mile in the 1930s; only one other street was more profitable it was said and that was Oxford Street, W.1. There was the post office, Sainsbury's Food Store, Boots the Chemist, the Co-operative, the Maypole, Liptons store, MacFisheries for fish and the Plaza Cinema which stick out in my mind. Although the market was always the centre of activity, on Saturday the market would remain open for business until 10.30 p.m. After dark, the stalls lit by oil lanterns hanging above the wares illuminated all the goods for sale. On Wednesday there was a livestock market, a few cows often getting loose and being chased up the road. The streets were lit by gas light, a man coming round every day to put them on in the evening and returning to put them off again in the morning. In the years before the 1939 war I remember being able to buy sweets for a farthing, the shopkeeper would hand them over the counter in a paper cone made of newspaper.

Judy Smith (*née*) Watters

Rhoda Smith in the third row standing third from left, wearing gloves in shoulder epaulet, at the inauguration of the Salvation Army life-saving guards. Captain Kingett and Lt Humphrey standing, 18 July 1921. (Sheila Acres)

A portable record player to take on trips in the great outdoors, 1920s. (Sheila Acres)

Carnival capers – Oliver Smith the bride, Ruby Smith the groom and Olive Smith, the pastor, 1930s. (Sheila Acres)

Another carnival procession, with Shire horses from the Romford Brewery Co. Sheila Acres standing alongside, 1980s. (Sheila Acres)

Wild-Eyed Animals

I remember growing up in Romford during the immediate post-war years, at that time more Essex than London, my earliest memories include the cattle market with its attendant assault on the senses. Walking down to St Edwards School on a fine Wednesday morning in early summer, sometimes meant loitering behind a heard of steaming, bellowing cattle, driven before man and dog towards the market. Wild eyed, sometimes lunging and surging, they moved inexorably towards the mêlée of animals and people at the bottom of the hill. Occasionally one frantic animal would break away from the herd and corner equally frantic wild-eyed shoppers in one of the doorways of Stones department store. Later in the day, the combination of noise and smell would become almost overpowering but the image at the end of the afternoon would be of a comparatively empty market except for the booted men with aprons and powerful hoses and straw-laden streams of tan-coloured water rushing towards the gulping drains along cobbled gutters.

Louis Roskell

Market Memories

As a child in the 1920s I remember the Market Place and being fascinated by the stalls loaded with an array of goodies, they traded until after dark, the stalls illuminated by Tilly lamps, the goods twinkling in the chill air at Christmastime. Although there was never much money to spare, Christmas was endowed with a magical atmosphere, we always had a little stocking and there was always an excitement in the air. The food on our table was never lacking and mother was a genius with provision of the festive fare together with her all year round excellent home-made pies, puddings and cakes. As a widow with limited income mother managed everything wonderfully well.

Ethel Whitehead (*née*) Shelley

Empire Day

Prior to the outbreak of war in 1939 Empire Day, 24 May, was a national holiday, schools were granted a half holiday in the afternoon to celebrate. Many children wore their wolf-cub or lifebuoy uniforms to school and carried Union Jack flags in preparation for the Empire Day pageant at Raphael Park in the afternoon. The cubs and lifebuoys were great rivals, which resulted in a fight breaking out between the two groups, hitting each other over the head with their Union Jacks in the school playground to demonstrate their patriotic enthusiasm for the British Empire.

John Strudwick

Injustice Corrected

While I was at Moss Lane Infants' School there was a Red Cross appeal for books for our prisoners of war. As encouragement we were offered a coloured cardboard medallion with an army rank printed on it dependent on number of books donated. One book for a private,

A popular pastime – a run out in the car for a picnic feast, 1920s. (Lesley Godbold)

right through seventeen army ranks to make you a field marshal, my carrier bag heavy with twenty-five of mother's unwanted books was presented in anticipation of appropriate reward. Miss Howship, our headmistress, could not have known about the system. Imagine my disappointment when I was handed a mere sergeant medallion for all those books! At the tender age of five I dared not challenge authority but I did complain to my mother, who, wise soul, advised me to take my problem straight to Miss Howship who had made the mistake. This I did, and the head was very understanding and in no time, I was a field marshal! My mother had taught me a very important lesson in life.

David Clark

The Seaside

As well as trains, two buses left Romford for the resort of Southend-on-Sea. Waiting at the bus stop outside St Edward's Church a tremendous sense of anticipation as the City coach emerged from North Street. In chocolate-coloured livery the streamlined monster shuddered rhythmically as we boarded and mother winced as I tried the enamel of my teeth against the vibrating chromium rail of the seat in front. It then made its majestic way via Brentwood and Billericay, the Westcliff-on-Sea No. 2A took the southerly route via Upminster. Southend was another dimension, used to the low perspective of my home ground my first visit saw a glittering silver wall rising up in front of me at the end of the street, which on closer inspection was found to be the sea. Generations of Londoners have experienced the hurly burly of resolute

The *Southend Belle* paddle steamer sets out fully loaded with day trippers, 1930s. (Sheila Acres)

A brewery outing in the charabanc for a day at the seaside, 1920s. (Sheila Acres)

enjoyment that was Southend. The sights and sounds, the smell of sausage and mash but settling for fish and chips, a boat trip around the wrecks, a walk to the end of the pier, a ride back on the tramway, tea and cakes at Garons, then back to the bus station for the long ride home!

Louis Roskell

Parachute Silk

I remember going to dances in Romford on my bicycle wearing my steel helmet which somebody had obtained for me. I learned to dance at the Nimbus Ballroom and used to go regularly to the dances at the Kings Head Hall, both in Market Place; after the last waltz, escorted home decorously by my current boyfriend. Once or twice a neighbour serving as a WAAF took me to the dances at RAF Hornchurch. There was a clothing shortage in the shops, but that did not worry us much. What we did look for however was silk from the parachutes of unexploded parachute mines or a downed airman. Parachute silk somehow found a way into

Smartly dressed for a stroll along the prom – stepping out at Southend, 1930s. (Ellen Preston)

The dedicated followers of fashion, 1931. (Sheila Acres)

the shops and was very much in demand, even in the post-war days of prolonged rationing. You could always find a dressmaker who would convert it into underwear or even bridal gowns. In 1943 I enlisted in the ATS.

Margaret Pollitt

Yes! We have no Bananas

This was the title of a popular song during the Second World War but I had no real idea of the meaning of the lyric or any knowledge of the fruit itself. It was not until nearly the end of the war that my mother managed to buy a small bunch from a local shop and offered me one. I had no idea how to progress with this prize, how to eat it or how to peel it, which caused my mother great amusement. At last she showed me how it must be 'unzipped' then what a disappointment for me as I tasted my first banana, I had expected it to be juicy like an orange which I had already tried previously, it was a long time after that first try before I actually ate another!

Ron Fuller

Oldchurch Hospital

My earliest memory of the old Oldchurch Hospital was undergoing a tonsillectomy there when I was about five years old. My next visit to the hospital was early in 1945 for appendicitis, which turned to peritonitis, necessitating a stay of three weeks. This was during the V1 flying bomb, and the V2 rocket raids affecting Romford and I was in a ward full of wounded troops from the invasion of Europe and was operated on by an army doctor! Later in the 1960s my sister, Margaret, did her nursing training at Oldchurch which was a teaching hospital. In June 2008 a reunion of student nurses and others took place, which will be bitter sweet as they remember the Oldchurch years, at a time when the hospital has been replaced by the Queens Hospital and the former Oldchurch Hospital has been demolished.

John Strudwick

Only Girl

The daughter of a Scout master and a Cub mistress who devoted themselves to assist youngsters growing up in the scouting traditions, it followed that from the age of four I joined scout camps! My memories are strong of singing songs around the campfire, ghost stories being told and so many adventures. The scouts at one time rescued me from a bog by forming a human chain and I safely emerged covered in mud. We encountered many summer storms, sought shelter in a pub and resorted to find sanctuary in school dormitories in Suffolk. Horses jumped fences and raided our tent with our food supplies for the week and caused chaos. It was great fun to be the only girl allowed to experience a boy's Scout camp!

Lesley Godbold (*née*) Gage

Marjorie and Alfred Gage, scoutmaster and cub mistress, gave many Romford youngsters good care, a great time and a good example in 1935. (Lesley Godbold)

Weekend camp at Waterholes Farm, Navestock. Eager Scouts transported all the required gear by walking with the scout handcart to the campsite. (Lesley Godbold)

First Romford Scouts. Alf (Gadget) Gage in the foreground. Behind, left to right: Dave (Gino) Watkins, Keith English, Bob Gildersleeve. (Lesley Godbold)

Peterkin Club

In the 1940s, The *Romford Recorder* used to run a children's column called the Peterkin Club, which was presided over by Uncle Peter. My brother, John, and I were enthusiastic members and went in for essay and painting competitions and contributed pieces about our pets and wildlife in the garden. Then came the 1948 Peterkin Club Christmas party held in the Wykeham Hall in the Market Place, where at last we would be meeting Uncle Peter himself. When he appeared, John and I marched up to him, introduced ourselves and mentioned a few things that we had contributed and that he had commented on in his column. He looked uncomprehendingly at us and appeared to be wishing that he would rather be anywhere but in the Wykeham Hall with a crowd of excited kids! He obviously was not Uncle Peter. John and I reported to Dad, who had previously told us that he had met Uncle Peter. Dad had to come clean and admit the 'Uncle Peter' was, in fact, one of the secretaries at the *Recorder* offices who ran the column. My brother and I resigned in disgust, but sixty years later, I would like to thank that unknown secretary who gave we Peterkins such a lot of pleasure.

David Clark

Coronation Day

2 June 1953, Coronation Day was a great day in Cromer Road where my parents were one of the few to own a television set – adult neighbours and friends were invited in to watch the ceremony. From early morning they arrived until our lounge was filled, five or six deep, sitting on the floor, on chairs, on the table and standing! The service seemed to go on for ages so for my brother and I it was more interesting to go out to play, after all we had a celebration party to go to in the afternoon. During the day the rain started so our party, instead of being held in the street, was transferred to a covered area in the garden of the local grocery store. A small stage was built where the children put on a talent show. I remember singing a duet with my friend Maureen Brown. We all had tea and were presented with sweets and a Coronation mug as we left.

Lesley Godbold (*née*) Gage

Leader of the Band

Aged nine I was mascot for the sea cadets and representing 'the senior service' I led a huge parade from Hornchurch into Romford. Proudly marching to Market Place, crowds watching and representatives of every kind of service joining our ranks along the way. My blunder was marching straight up North Street, instead of turning right at the Market Place towards the war memorial and Raphael's Park. Only my own band followed, we

Sea Cadet mascot Pound aged nine years, the leader of the band, 1946. (Pound Family)

The Remembrance Day Parade, 1946. The Senior Service Sea Cadets lead the way into Romford. (Pound Family)

had to rectify matters by racing through alleyways to reclaim our place at the head of the procession! Not easy for the drummers and the buglers were puffed out, a 'Remembrance Day' I cannot forget.

Birger Pound

Mawney Road Baths

My brother, Ron Wilson, emigrated to America in 1957 and many years later, whilst working in his office a new colleague approached him, explaining he had heard he came from England and enquired if he knew of Romford in Essex. Ron confirmed it was his birthplace. The man explained that as a GI during the war he was stationed in Exeter, Devon, and in an antique shop had bought a silver trowel. The inscription confirmed the trowel had been used to lay the foundation stone of the Mawney Road Swimming Baths, Romford. Ron showed a scar on his chin received from jumping in backwards at the pool and could also boast it was where he had learnt to swim. Ron was allowed to bring the trowel home on his next visit and the *Romford Recorder* ran an article and took photographs of him holding the trowel outside the baths, before returning it to the USA. What a story, once again proving life can be stranger than fiction! The swimming baths have since been demolished but my whole family have fond memories of the pool as all my brothers and sisters learned to swim there, all six of us!

Hilda Bennett (*née*) Wilson

Ron Wilson holding the trowel used for the laying of the foundation stone at Mawney Road swimming bath. He brought it back on a visit to Romford with a strange tale from the USA. (Reprinted courtesy *Romford Recorder*)

The Betting Shop

Betting shops became legal on 1 May 1961 and one of the first to open in Romford was George Brent, a small shop at the top of the Market Place. On market days, especially Wednesday and Saturday from 2 p.m. this small shop would be packed with a wide range of people and some fascinating characters. As the afternoon wore on it would become more crowded with many market stallholders coming in with their takings to risk on the horses. By this time most people had been smoking, either for pleasure or anxiety and the smoke so thick it hung in the air just above head height. A commentary on each race came over a tannoy system and during the race a crescendo of noise with everyone shouting the horses on. During the afternoon there was a great camaraderie amongst the punters, but at the end of the day there were a few happy faces leaving the shop and many more unhappy faces as they had lost most of their hard-earned money. But the same faces would be back the following week with high hopes of making their fortune.

Ron Fuller

Gasworks Outing

My grandad and my father worked at the Romford Gasworks throughout their working lives and they both looked forward to the annual outing to the seaside, which often they would enjoy together in the years when they both worked there. In 1924 the destination

The Gasworks outing took a charabanc ride to Brighton at 12mph in 1924. Grandad Meekings and his son 'Bill' are seated together mid-point just above the sign on the door, Perry's of Ilford. (Roy Meekings)

was Brighton and along with colleagues they would clamber aboard the mighty charabanc that would transport them to the seaside at the sedate top speed of 12mph! Consequently they left at 4 a.m. on their jaunt, finally arriving at their destination, it seems they would take up residence in a public house until 'last orders' and trundle home again arriving in Romford at 5 a.m. next day. Well it seems they enjoyed this gad about but then it was back to the place of work until the next time. In retirement Grandad received a concessionary allowance for gas light in his home in Marks Road, long after most people were using electricity in the home he doggedly insisted to continue to enjoy this benefit from his former employer.

Roy Meekings

Hot Sausage Roll

Memories of Romford for me include going shopping to the market with my mother and always as a special treat we would go to Taylor's the butcher in North Street and she would buy me a delicious hot sausage roll, I can still remember the taste even now. One side of the shop was selling beef and the other pork meat and they made their own sausage rolls! This was a reward after mother had visited some of her favourite stalls – there was Jack, who sold leather shoes, Harry, selling leather purses and handbags, and Lou, who sold everything in 'old money'. After we had gone 'metric' he would talk of 'two bob', 'half-a-crown', 'shillings' and 'tanners'.

Lou was very amusing – he would perform for the crowd and use the phrases, 'I won't ask a fiver, go on give me a pound.' My father too often took me to the market and let me spend ages looking at the kittens and puppies for sale there.

Ellen Preston (née) Huggett

Guy Fawkes

We would look forward to 5 November every year and while at Mawney Road School Infant and Junior Schools joined Izzit's fireworks club, this was at a sweet shop opposite the school. Every week we paid in our pocket-money pennies to the club so when the great day dawned we showed our membership cards with our payments recorded and purchased our fireworks, Chinese crackers, sparklers, Catherine wheels, rockets etc. We also made dummies of Guy Fawkes with a placard attached reading 'spare a penny for the guy'; this was outside our house in the hope of more pennies. The effigy was burnt amid a firework display, to commemorate the unmasking of the gunpowder plot to blow up the Houses of Parliament in 1605.

John Strudwick

Irish Guard

My husband Bill did National Service with the Irish Guards; he served with great pride with a wonderful group of men, their uniform world famous because of royal connections. The changing of the guard at Buckingham Palace is a sight not to be missed by tourists visiting London from around the globe. Bill undertook royal duties connected with the funerals of

Irish Guardsman, Bill Acres, wearing his uniform with pride. (Sheila Acres)

1951 Sgt J. Cave's Squad, Irish Guards at the guards' depot. Mr Acres is standing extreme right in middle row. (Bill Acres)

The daughters of Sheila and Bill Acres are presented to the Queen Mother at St Patrick's Day celebrations – note the shamrock in the officer's cap. (Bill Acres)

both Queen Mary and her son King George VI, the Coronation of Queen Elizabeth II and the Trooping of the Colour. We married at St Andrew's Church and celebrated our golden wedding in 2005 and I have spent all my life in Romford. Our two daughters were keen members of Romford Drum and Trumpet Band and we enjoyed travelling with them at home and abroad, lending support when our local band was in competition.

Sheila Acres (née) Sallows

Monday Wash

Monday was always 'washing day' for mother – in fine weather things would go out on the line, if the weather was inclement the drying took place in the kitchen. A great 'copper' would come into play on wash day with a scrubbing board playing a part. I remember too this 'blue' which was also essential which I am advised was called 'Reckitts' blue, contained and bound up in a little pack the size of a cotton reel, it was some form of whitening agent. The process would not be complete until everything had been offered to the mangle before drying commenced. When dry, the piles of ironing were tackled – my mother always amazed us as she was a wonderful housekeeper in spite of her blindness, and her ironing skills were another never to be forgotten event. She always did the ironing on a scrubbed-deal tabletop, suitably covered for the ironing and had three different cast-iron irons heating on the big black cast-iron oven range. She would skilfully hold the iron up very close to

Another reason for pride – the internationally famous Romford Drum and Trumpet Corps Band, started in 1957 celebrated a golden fifty years in 2007. (Sheila Acres)

The Romford Drum and Trumpet Corps Band proudly display some of their many prizes and trophies. (Sheila Acres)

her face to assess if the heat was right for the intended job. That black oven always polished bright with 'Zebo' and a set of brushes. Gas mantels either side of the mantel, which was decorated with fabric hung from brass-headed pins, and this above a big wire fireguard surrounding the hearth. As a matter of interest this same washday copper I mentioned was used to cook our Christmas pudding! When it was bath night a galvanised bath would find a way into the scullery from the garden shed, with linoleum as floor covering and harsh coconut matting on top this was not particularly comfortable. The gas stove provided the hot water and more was added as bathing progressed. There was always 'an order of the bath' my younger brother Dennis first, then my turn, then father and lastly the socks!

Tony Castleton

My Mother

My mother Ann, one of eight children, the youngest daughter of a happy family in Stepney, her childhood filled with older siblings, great times but few luxuries. A born raconteur, I loved to hear stories from her early years, troubled by a desire to use her left hand, unacceptable at the time, she persevered to write with her right hand but always considered this an injustice. Similarly, a swimming teacher who pushed non-swimmers into the pool deprived her of confidence in water and she never learnt to swim. She always maintained her sense of humour,

Pretty maids all in a row – a first-communion day group at St Edward's R.C. Church.

had a rich singing voice and with brother Dick won many dance contests. She encouraged all her children in all their talents and was so proud when my partner and I danced at the Royal Albert Hall for the International Dancing Masters Association. I attended the City of London School for Girls and the wheel of fortune had turned full circle – I could write with whichever hand I wanted! Mother married my father in August 1933 and their one-day honeymoon was at Southend. They moved to Romford having been bombed out in London and Charlie started a new business selling fish in the market and the rest as they say is history. I remember my mother with a strong sense of fair play, with many wonderful qualities, very wise and kind. On her forty-fourth birthday I was born, her only daughter.

Annette Butterworth (*née*) Fancourt

Oldchurch Entrance

In the early hours of a snowy February morning in 1936 I was born at Oldchurch Hospital and was named after the midwife who hailed from Scotland. Like so many others who arrived and made their first appearance in this hospital, I was very sorry to learn that this venerable building has been demolished. During the years of my growing up, I remember the family liked nothing better than to go to Romford Market to shop on a Saturday. I remember the animals and that the pens languished there long after animal sales ceased in the late fifties. When my father returned home after the war, he would take the family to Taylor's Restaurant in North Street as a treat, where many a fine lunch was enjoyed.

Jean Pound (*née*) Williams

Roy Meekings, with white open-necked shirt and attaché case ready for the seaside outing, 1952.

Returning Bottles

When we lived in the cottages in Waterloo Road overlooking the brewery yard, from my bedroom window I would often watch grandad at work busy on one chore or another. In those days the brewery was a hive of industry and the lorries would continuously drive in and out of the yard with their loads, either fully loaded with beer or with empty returns for reuse, so you see recycling bottles is not a new idea. In fact as a child I remember all beer bottles carried a deposit and two pennies refund on return was an incentive to take the bottles back to the off licence. Many bottles carried such a promise at point of sale including jam-jar returns. Children were often very keen to undertake the job of returning empties and pocketing the pennies if allowed, to convert to money for sweets.

Sheila Acres (*née*) Sallows

Wondering Still

When very young during the Second World War I recall my grandmother lifting me up to see a plane flying low over the arterial road (A127) when suddenly she realised it was an enemy plane. I remember seeing the black-cross markings and also the fact that the pilot gave us a friendly wave. I have often wondered if he survived the war and because of this gesture I always rather hoped he had.

Patrick Arnold

Neighbourhood Fun

One of my vivid memories from my childhood during the 1950s concerns children's outings, arranged to take groups of children off for the day to Southend or Clacton-on-Sea on the Essex coast. A Mrs Finch arranged these outings for the children living in Rush Green Road, Clayton Road, Bellhouse Road and Meadow Road. Can you imagine what a special treat we children thought this was, a 'blue-ribbon day' of great excitement as we set off for a day at the seaside. Those efforts of Mrs Finch and all the mothers to see their children did not miss out on this great expedition can only now be properly appreciated. Mothers of the neighbourhood all co-operating and working together to bring this bit of fun into their children's lives. The coach would arrive to transport us to the world of buckets and spades, ice cream and seaside rock. What a difference today, for as I write, my wife and I now both enjoying retirement, are just returned from a splendid cruise around the world. But included in my memory box, among the wonderful sights this journey has offered, there will remain one little spot where the joy of those first visits to the seaside will always remain.

Roy Meekings

Other local titles published by The History Press

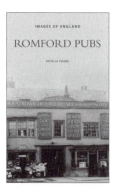

Romford Pubs
PATRICIA POUND

Using archive photographs and advertisements, this selection relates the history of Romford's many pubs, from the days when they were filled with agricultural workers and gentlemen drinkers (and the occasional dentist or doctor plying his trade) to the pool tables and cigarette machines of today's establishments. With archive images of Victorian brewery workers and the temperance mission in Brazier's Yard, the brewery football team of the 1940s, the laboratories of the 1960s and the final end of Romford's brewing days in 1993, *Romford Pubs* provides a fascinating and comprehensive history of brewing in the town.

978 0 7524 3841 2

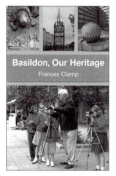

Basildon, Our Heritage
FRANCES CLAMP

The Basildon Heritage Project worked with children from five local primary schools who were introduced to digital cameras and used their new skills in helping to establish the Basildon Heritage Trail, a journey around many points of local interest. The photographs used in the book compliment the story of Basildon. Each of the five schools has its own unique tale to tell. The children are the future of the town and their involvement in the making of the trail and this book has made them more aware of their valuable heritage.

978 0 7524 4551 9

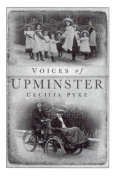

Voices of Upminster
CECILIA PYKE

Upminster is a leafy suburb of London which has seen many changes over the last century. In this delightful collection of memories, local writer and long-term resident Cecilia Pyke has asked a range of people about living and working in the area. Complemeteed by 100 photographs from the author's and residents' private collections, this glimpse into the past will bring back nostalgic memories for some and reveal surprises for others as they visit the past through other people's eyes.

978 0 7524 4556 4

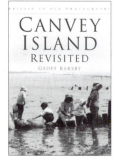

Canvey Island Revisited
GEOFF BARSBY

Sitting just off the Essex coast and surrounded by water on all sides, Canvey Island's location has contributed to its intriguing past. Following on from the first two collections of archive images, this new volume revisits the Canvey Island of yesteryear with 200 fascinating photographs, postcards and other ephemera. *Canvey Island Revisited* is an important pictorial history that will be of interest to all those who have ever lived in or visited the area.

978 0 7524 3984 6

If you are interested in purchasing other books published by The History Press, or in case you have difficulty finding any History Press books in your local bookshop, you can also place orders directly through our website

www.thehistorypress.co.uk